OPPOSING
VIEWPOINTS®
SERIES

Religion and Sexuality

Other Books of Related Interest:

Opposing Viewpoints Series

Reproductive Technologies

Current Controversies Series

The Abortion Controversy

Homosexuality

"Congress shall make no law . . . abridging the freedom of speech, or of the press."

First Amendment to the U.S. Constitution

The basic foundation of our democracy is the First Amendment guarantee of freedom of expression. The Opposing Viewpoints series is dedicated to the concept of this basic freedom and the idea that it is more important to practice it than to enshrine it.

OPPOSING
VIEWPOINTS®
SERIES

Religion and Sexuality

Kevin Hillstrom, Book Editor

GREENHAVEN PRESS

An imprint of Thomson Gale, a part of The Thomson Corporation

THOMSON
———✳———™
GALE

Detroit • New York • San Francisco • New Haven, Conn. • Waterville, Maine • London

Christine Nasso, *Publisher*
Elizabeth Des Chenes, *Managing Editor*

LIBRARY OF CONGRESS CATALOGING-IN-PUBLICATION DATA

Religion and sexuality / Kevin Hillstrom, book editor.
    p. cm. -- Opposing Viewpoints
Includes bibliographical references and index.
ISBN-13: 978-0-7377-3749-3 (hardcover)
ISBN-13: 978-0-7377-3750-9 (pbk.)
ISBN-10: 0-7377-3750-6
1. Sex--Religious aspects. 2. Homosexuality--Religious aspects. 3. Birth control--Religious aspects. 4. Religious leaders--Sexual behavior. I. Hillstrom, Kevin, 1963-
HQ63.R45 2008
205'.66--dc22
                                        2007025661

ISBN-10: 0-7377-3749-2
ISBN-10: 0-7377-3749-2

Printed in the United States of America
10 9 8 7 6 5 4 3 2 1

Contents

Chapter 3: Is a Belief in God Incompatible with Reproductive Rights?

Chapter 4: What Issues of Sexuality Surround Religious Leaders?

Why Consider
Opposing Viewpoints?

> *"The only way in which a human being can make some approach to knowing the whole of a subject is by hearing what can be said about it by persons of every variety of opinion and studying all modes in which it can be looked at by every character of mind. No wise man ever acquired his wisdom in any mode but this."*
>
> *John Stuart Mill*

In our media-intensive culture it is not difficult to find differing opinions. Thousands of newspapers and magazines and dozens of radio and television talk shows resound with differing points of view. The difficulty lies in deciding which opinion to agree with and which "experts" seem the most credible. The more inundated we become with differing opinions and claims, the more essential it is to hone critical reading and thinking skills to evaluate these ideas. Opposing Viewpoints books address this problem directly by presenting stimulating debates that can be used to enhance and teach these skills. The varied opinions contained in each book examine many different aspects of a single issue. While examining these conveniently edited opposing views, readers can develop critical thinking skills such as the ability to compare and contrast authors' credibility, facts, argumentation styles, use of persuasive techniques, and other stylistic tools. In short, the Opposing Viewpoints series is an ideal way to attain the higher-level thinking and reading skills so essential in a culture of diverse and contradictory opinions.

In addition to providing a tool for critical thinking, Opposing Viewpoints books challenge readers to question their own strongly held opinions and assumptions. Most people form their opinions on the basis of upbringing; peer pressure; and personal, cultural, or professional bias. By reading carefully balanced opposing views, readers must directly confront new ideas as well as the opinions of those with whom they disagree. This is not to simplistically argue that everyone who reads opposing views will—or should—change his or her opinion. Instead, the series enhances readers' understanding of their own views by encouraging confrontation with opposing ideas. Careful examination of others' views can lead to the readers' understanding of the logical inconsistencies in their own opinions, perspective on why they hold an opinion, and consideration of the possibility that their opinion requires further evaluation.

Evaluating Other Opinions

To ensure that this type of examination occurs, Opposing Viewpoints books present all types of opinions. Prominent spokespeople on different sides of each issue as well as well-known professionals from many disciplines challenge the reader. An additional goal of the series is to provide a forum for other, less-known, or even unpopular viewpoints. The opinion of an ordinary person who has had to make the decision to cut off life support from a terminally ill relative, for example, may be just as valuable and provide just as much insight as a medical ethicist's professional opinion. The editors have two additional purposes in including these less-known views. One, the editors encourage readers to respect others' opinions—even when not enhanced by professional credibility. It is only by reading or listening to and objectively evaluating others' ideas that one can determine whether they are worthy of consideration. Two, the inclusion of such viewpoints encourages the important critical thinking skill of objectively evaluating an author's credentials and bias. This evaluation will illuminate an author's reasons for taking a particular stance on an issue and will aid in readers' evaluation of the author's ideas.

It is our hope that these books will give readers a deeper understanding of the issues debated and an appreciation of the complexity of even seemingly simple issues when good and honest people disagree. This awareness is particularly important in a democratic society such as ours in which people enter into public debate to determine the common good. Those with whom one disagrees should not be regarded as enemies but rather as people whose views deserve careful examination and may shed light on one's own.

Thomas Jefferson once said that "difference of opinion leads to inquiry, and inquiry to truth." Jefferson, a broadly educated man, argued that "if a nation expects to be ignorant and free . . . it expects what never was and never will be." As individuals and as a nation, it is imperative that we consider the opinions of others and examine them with skill and discernment. The Opposing Viewpoints series is intended to help readers achieve this goal.

David L. Bender and Bruno Leone,
Founders

Introduction

> "Sexual intimacy within God's boundaries of a loving, committed marriage can provide tremendous joy and fun; it can celebrate intimacy and love; it can bring the blessing of children; and it can create and sustain the mysterious and sacred oneness of marriage. But if you let it burn outside of God's boundaries, it becomes a self-serving act that can and will destroy careers, marriages, children, reputations, and even life itself. . . . When sexual release is pursued outside of the one-man, one-woman sexual celebration of marriage, then the sacredness of sex is violated. The very heart of this holy union is broken."
>
> —Tim A. Gardner,
> Christian counselor
> Sacred Sex

> "We have many voices today . . . insisting that theology deal more seriously with actual human sexual experience. . . . My hope is that out of these struggles in sexual theology, an ethic might increasingly emerge that will have several marks. It will be strongly sex-affirming, understanding sexual pleasure as a moral good rooted in the sacred value of our sensuality and erotic power, and not needing justification by procreative possibility. It will be grounded in respect for our own and others' bodily integrity . . .

It will celebrate fidelity in our commitments without legalistic prescription as to the precise forms such fidelity must make. It will be an ethic whose principles apply equally and without double standards to persons of both genders, of all colors, ages, bodily conditions, and sexual orientations."

—James Nelson,
Theologian
Body Theology

Major world religions, including Islam, Judaism, Buddhism, Hinduism, and Christianity, provide ethical guidelines and tenets about human sexuality and sexual behavior. Many of these guidelines can be found in the leading holy books of these religions, such as the Qur'an, the Torah, and the New Testament. But even among devoted adherents to these religions, deep tensions and differences exist when it comes to the issue of sex. People of the same faith consult the same holy scriptures for guidance about sexual practice and sexual morality, only to reach remarkably different conclusions about how they and other members of society should behave. For example, some people interpret their holy texts literally because they believe that the authors were directly inspired by God. Others approach these same texts with the conviction that the authors of these books expressed current religious beliefs and tenets and did not intend to provide a literal account of events.

Theologians, religious leaders, and laity also differ in what they *emphasize* when they study their holy texts for guidance or inspiration. For example, Christian opponents of homosexuality and same-sex marriage often quote Biblical passages such as Leviticus 18:22, which states that "You shall not lie with a man as with a woman; it is an abomination" punishable by execution. By contrast, liberal Christians (as well as nonbelievers who are supportive of gay rights) emphasize biblical scriptures that advocate inclusion, love, and acceptance. They also seize on other scriptural passages about sexuality that are often ignored by others, such as Deuteronomy 22:13–21, which commands that if a new bride is discovered to not be a virgin, she should be immediately stoned to death.

Each side of the heated debates over homosexuality and gay rights thus enters the fray with plenty of scriptural argument to support its position. But the resulting clamor can make it difficult to establish even a fragile dialogue, let alone find common spiritual ground.

This hotly debated issue is but one of several located at the intersection of American attitudes about religion and sexuality that are discussed in the following chapters: How Do Religious Beliefs Shape Sexual Behavior? Should Homosexuality Be Condemned on Religious Grounds? Is a Belief in God Incompatible with Reproductive Rights? and What Issues of Sexuality Surround Religious Leaders? The widely divergent answers to these questions found in the pages that follow provide evidence of the deep divisions that run through American society on the subjects of sex and religion. Many of these views appear to be fixed and unchangeable, but at a minimum this presentation encourages people to critically examine their assumptions and beliefs—and perhaps it will help people on various sides of these issues to gain a greater understanding of deeply held beliefs that run counter to their own.

OPPOSING
VIEWPOINTS®
SERIES

CHAPTER 1

How Do Religious Beliefs Shape Sexual Behavior?

Chapter Preface

Advocates and opponents of sexual activity outside of traditional marriage truly do see the world differently. As a result, the various positions seek to establish their own definitions of the issues—and stakes—involved when people engage in premarital sex. Proponents of premarital sex insist that as long as one's sexual partner is treated with respect and precautions are taken to address concerns about sexually transmitted diseases and unintended pregnancy, engaging in sex outside of marriage is morally defensible. In fact, many people who engage in premarital sex claim that their sexual activities reflect their determination to fully experience all that life has to offer, including exploring emotional intimacy with others and savoring the gift of bodily pleasure bestowed by God.

Opposition to sexual activity outside of traditional marriage is based in part on concerns about AIDS and other sexually transmitted diseases as well as unplanned pregnancies. But a great deal of the criticism of premarital sex is grounded in religious convictions. According to these critics, Bible teachings clearly stipulate that sex outside of marriage is, by definition, a moral wrong. People who hold this view believe that sexually active single people use rationalizations about their motivations as a way to excuse morally reprehensible behavior. Advocates of abstinence assert that the only sexual activity sanctioned by God occurs within marriage.

Few observers believe that the philosophical chasm between these two camps will be bridged any time soon. But both sides agree that religious beliefs are frequently the single most decisive factors in determining to which position a person will ultimately adhere. Studies indicate, for example, that teens from actively religious families and with friends who regularly attend religious services tend to have sex at later ages compared to teens whose parents and friends do not have strong religious beliefs. As the viewpoints in this chapter indicate, the two sides have profoundly different perspectives on what lessons this information holds for U.S. society as a whole.

"I wanted someone to explain to me that I could be a faithful Christian and blithely continue having premarital sex. But in the end, I was never able to square sex outside of marriage with the Christian story about God, redemption, and human bodies."

Sex Is Intended for Traditional Marriage

Lauren F. Winner

In this viewpoint, Lauren F. Winner, a Christian essayist, author, and former book editor for Beliefnet, *explains why she believes that God intends for sex only to be practiced within the institution of marriage. She acknowledges that modern American culture is drenched with messages that encourage sexual permissiveness, but she claims that the Book of Genesis and the New Testament epistles of the apostle Paul make it clear God intended people to engage in sex only within marriage.*

Lauren F. Winner, *Real Sex: The Naked Truth About Chastity*. Ada, MI: Brazos Press, 2005, pp. 29–31, 32–34, 35–39, 40, 41–42. Copyright © 2005 by Lauren F. Winner. Reproduced by permission.

As you read, consider the following questions:

1. How does Winner use the story of Adam and Eve to make her point that even though human bodies are good, "it does not follow that everything bodies do is good"?

2. According to the author, how is sex outside marriage similar to Walt Disney's Wilderness Lodge Resort?

3. What is the name of the poem found in Hebrew scripture that is cited by the author as the "perfect expression" of sexuality as intended by God?

The bottom line is this: God created sex for marriage, and within a Christian moral vocabulary, it is impossible to defend sex outside of marriage. To more liberal readers, schooled on a generation of Christian ethics written in the wake of the sexual revolution, this may sound like old-fashioned hooey, but it is the simple, if sometimes difficult, truth.

For several years, I tried and tried to find a way to wiggle out of the church's traditional teaching that God requires chastity outside of marriage, and I failed. I read all the classics of 1970s Christian sexual ethics, all the appealing and comforting books that insisted that Christians must avoid not sex outside of marriage, but rather exploitative sex, or sex where you run the risk of getting hurt. These books suggest that it is not marriage per se, but rather the intent or state of mind of the people involved, that determines whether or not sex is good and appropriate; if a man and woman love each other, if they are committed to each other, or, for Pete's sake, if they are just honest with each other about their fling being a no-strings-attached, one-night stand, then sex between them is just fine. After all, as long as our 1970s man and woman care about each other, making love will be meaningful. In fact, sex might even liberate them, or facilitate their personal development.

Searching for Answers

Well. I tried to find these books persuasive. I wanted to find them persuasive. I wanted someone to explain to me that I could be a faithful Christian and blithely continue having premarital sex. But in the end, I was never able to square sex outside of marriage with the Christian story about God, redemption, and human bodies.

It wasn't just the liberal, supposedly liberating, books that left me cold. I didn't find many of the more conservative bromides all that persuasive either—the easy proof-texting that purports to draw a coherent sexual ethic from a few verses of Paul. To be sure, scripture has plenty to teach us about how rightly to order our sexual lives, but, as the church, we need to ask whether the starting point for a scriptural witness on sex is the isolated quotation of "thou shalt not," or whether a scriptural ethic of sex begins instead with the totality of the Bible, the narrative of God's redeeming love and humanity's attempt to reflect that through our institutions and practices. If our aim is to construct a rule book, perhaps the cut-and-paste approach to scripture is adequate: as the bumper sticker wisdom goes, *Jesus* (or in this case, Paul) *said it, I do it.* But if we see scripture not merely as a code of behavior but as a map of God's reality, and if we take seriously the pastoral task of helping unmarried Christians live chastely, the church needs not merely to recite decontextualized Bible verses, but to ground our ethic in the faithful living of the fullness of the gospel. As ethicist Thomas E. Breidenthal once put it, "We must do more than invoke the will of God if we wish to recover a viable Christian sexual morality. . . . Even if God's will is obvious, it cannot provide a rationale for any moral code until we are able to say, clearly and simply, how God's command speaks to us, how and why it addresses us not only as a demand but as good news.". . .

God's Vision of Sexuality

God made us with bodies; that is how we begin to know that He cares how we order our sexual lives. There is—and we will walk through it here—evidence aplenty from both scripture and tradition about how God intends sex, about where sex belongs and where it is disordered, about when sex is righteous and when it is sinful. But the starting point is this: God created us with bodies; God Himself incarnated in a human body; Jesus was raised again from the dead with a body; and one day we too will be resurrected with our bodies. That is the beginning of any Christian ethic—any moral theology—of how human beings in bodies interact with other bodies.

Sexuality touches every area of human life; even something as simple as a kiss can have social consequences (after The Kiss, you go from being the girl next door to being his girlfriend) and emotional consequences (you hadn't realized you liked him *that way* until then). Kisses can play on our psychological and spiritual registers. But sexuality, even mere kissing, is also, unavoidably, bodily. After all, we define a kiss by body parts: a kiss happens when lips meet a cheek or a hand, or when two sets of lips rub up against each other. Kissing can make our bodies tingle. And kisses can be slobbery; like other sexual deeds, they are messy in their embodiment.

So an investigation of God's vision for human sexuality would begin with God's vision for human bodies. And that investigation can be less simple than it seems. The Christian story, at its core, has very positive things to say about bodies, but throughout its history the church has sometimes equivocated. We Christians get embarrassed about our bodies. We are not always sure that God likes them very much. We are not sure whether bodies are good or bad; it follows that we are not sure whether sex is good or bad.

The Christian view of bodies—that is, God's view of bodies—cannot be abstracted from the biblical account of creation. God created people with bodies, and God declared that

23

they were good. It is sometimes hard for us modern-day Christians to grasp that central fact. Bodies are not simply pieces of furniture to decorate or display; they are not trappings about which we have conflicted feelings ("body images" that we need to revamp or retool); they are not objects to be dieted away, made to conform to popular standards, or made to perform unthinkable athletic feats with the help of drugs; they are neither tools for scoring points nor burdens to be overcome. They are simply good. A second-century Syrian Christian text, "The Odes of Solomon," can remind us of this basic truth. The speaker in the poem is God, and He is talking about human beings:

> I fashioned their members, and my own breasts I prepared for them,
>
> That they might drink my holy milk and live by it.
>
> I am pleased by them,
>
> And am not ashamed by them.
>
> For my workmanship are they,
>
> And the strength of my thoughts.

Sexual Desire and Sin

God's creation, including human bodies, is good, but it does not follow that everything bodies do is good. The next act of the Christian story is the fall—Adam and Eve disobey God and a great gulf grows between them and Him, a gulf signified by their being pushed out of the Garden. Indeed, it is interesting to note that sin entered the world through the bodily act of eating, and the consequences of the fall were telegraphed on human bodies—Adam would toil in physical labor, Eve would feel pain in childbirth and would desire her husband (a desire that can be understood as physical, emotional, and

God Can Not Be Removed from the Bedroom

Those who have chosen the full-libertarian agenda that God and ethics have nothing to do with the bedroom or reproduction have some tough questions to face. Are there any moral constraints at all on sexual or reproductive freedom? Is nothing morally required of us in matters of this quite significant part of human experience? Is one's "heart's desire" the trump card for all our decisions? One wonders what might be the source of the massive repression of compunction in priests who abused children, of teachers who seduced their students, of parents who violated their own. Surely such horrors have taken place for ages. But have they been done with such absence of guilt? And what of sex itself? Do the astounding profits in pornography, the mounting rates of sexually transmitted diseases, the images of pop and hip-hop music videos or the edgy offerings of the television and fashion industries offer any vision of sex that is even remotely connected to love, commitment or children?

John F. Kavanaugh, "Of Human Life," America,
vol. 194, no. 18, May 22, 2006.

spiritual), and both would die. Still, it would be an error to conclude that in a fallen world, everything bodies do is bad. Sexual desire is not, in itself, a wicked thing. Rather, in the fall, our sexual desires were disordered, and one task of Christian ethics is to help us rightly order them.

Genesis is only the starting point for understanding God's vision of the body. . . .

The most important—and also perhaps the most complex—figure in the articulation of a distinctively Christian understanding of the body is the apostle Paul. In his New Testament epistles, Paul meditates at length upon bodies. Paul is concerned with human bodies—what they are made of, what they are good for, and how Christians should inhabit them. He also uses the body as a theological metaphor that captures the essence of the Pauline understanding of the gospel. As Anglican theologian John A. T. Robinson eloquently put it, "The concept of the body forms the keystone of Paul's theology.... It is from the body of sin and death that we are delivered; it is through the body of Christ on the Cross that we are saved; it is into His body the Church that we are incorporated; it is by His body in the Eucharist that this Community is sustained; it is in our body that its new life is to be manifested; it is to a resurrection of this body to the likeness of His glorious body that we are destined." As Robinson notes, Paul encompasses almost all of the basics of Christian theology—humanity, sin, incarnation, atonement, ecclesiology, sacramentality, eschatology—in the single image of the body.

Christ and the Church

Paul assumes that his readers value and care for their own physical bodies. Indeed, when trying to explain to the Ephesians how much Christ loves the church, Paul draws an analogy between Christ's love and each person's love for his own body: "No one ever hated his own body; on the contrary, he keeps it nourished and warm, and that is how Christ treats the church, because it is his body, of which we are living parts." Paul takes for granted that bodies are good things, to be nourished and loved. He assumes his readers share his perspective and can begin to see that Christ tends to them just as carefully as they tend to their own bodies.

But Paul does not assume that bodies are morally neutral. He understands that bodies are the sites of longings and temptations, of desires that can sometimes trump reason and rectitude, of powers and passions that can be glorious but can also be dangerous. Bodies, Paul knows, are complicated. Though they were created good, their parts and impulses, their desires and leanings were corrupted in the fall, just as human emotions and human intellect were corrupted. It is hard for us moderns to hold Paul's two truths in tension. We want things to be clear-cut, yes or no, either/or. Bodies can be exploited; they can be destructive and dangerous. At the same time, bodies are good, as all of God's creation is good; and rightly ordered by a Christian moral vision, bodies are tools God uses for His glory. [religious historian Wayne] Meeks has captured the nuances of Paul's take on bodies. In Meeks's phrase, Paul insists that "what is done 'in the body' is morally significant"; however, Paul also maintains that "the human predicament is the result not of the limitations of physical existence, but of sin."

Bodies are central to the Christian story. Creation inaugurates bodies that are good, but the consequences of the fall are written on our bodies—our bodies will sweat as we labor in the fields, our bodies will hurt as we bear children, and, most centrally, our bodies will die. If the fall is written on the body, salvation happens in the body too. The kingdom of God is transmitted through Jesus's body and is sustained in Christ's Body, the church. Through the bodily suffering of Christ on the cross and the bodily resurrection of Christ from the dead, we are saved. Bodies are not just mirrors in which we see the consequence of the fall; they are also, in one theologian's phrase, "where God has chosen to find us in our fallenness." Bodies are who we are and where we live; they are not just things God created us with, but means of knowing Him and abiding with Him.

Sex and Genesis

Just as scripture's vision of bodies begins in Genesis, scripture's story about sex also begins in Genesis. God's vision for humanity is established in the Garden of Eden, and the uniqueness and one-ness of the marriage relationship between Adam and Eve is inaugurated in Genesis 1–2. In the first chapters of

Genesis, we learn that God created a relationship between Adam and Eve. This relationship is the context in which sex is first understood. In a graphic speech, Adam speaks of his and Eve's becoming one flesh. One-fleshness both is and is not metaphor. It captures an all-encompassing, overarching oneness—when they marry, husband and wife enter an institution that points them toward familial, domestic, emotional, and spiritual unity. But the one flesh of which Adam speaks is also overtly sexual, suggesting sexual intercourse, the only physical state other than pregnancy where it is hard to tell where one person's body stops and the other's starts.

This is why it is hard to discuss Christian sexual ethics abstracted from Christian social and marital ethics. When it comes to sex, one cannot leave out marriage. The *no* to sex outside marriage seems arbitrary and cruel apart from the Creator's *yes* to sex within marriage. Indeed, one can say that in Christianity's vocabulary the only real sex is the sex that happens in a marriage; the faux sex that goes on outside marriage is not really sex at all. The physical coming together that happens between two people who are not married is only a distorted imitation of sex, as Walt Disney's Wilderness Lodge Resort is only a simulation of real wilderness. The danger is that when we spend too much time in the simulations, we lose the capacity to distinguish between the ersatz and the real.

Even though we are fallen, we remain part of God's original creation. We were created in particular ways, with particular longings and desires and impulses. Those desires have become distorted in the fall, but they are still here within us, shaping our wants and our actions and our thoughts and our wishes. This is nowhere clearer than in human sexuality. The impulse for relationship with which God created humanity animates us—and powerful sexual desire is still with us, too. But one has only to flip through the pages of *Men's Health* or even glance at the nightly news to see that in contemporary society, men and women express sexual longings in all sorts of ways that are out of sync with God's vision of marital sex.

The Bible has something to say about all of this. The Bible understands what happened in the fall; and all the laws that biblical writers, from Moses to Paul, articulate are efforts to protect and perpetuate the ordering of things that was established in the Garden of Eden. The Mosaic laws about family relationships and sexual practices—even the faintly embarrassing and seemingly self-evident rules about avoiding incest and bestiality—do protective work, pointing to, guarding, and returning God's people to the created order, the world as God meant it to be. (Song of Songs, the erotic love poem found in Hebrew scripture, is the perfect expression of what this sexuality, restored by law and grace, looks like. It features a lover proclaiming to his beloved, "You are stately as a palm tree, and your breasts are like its clusters. . . . I will climb the palm tree and lay hold of its branches." The beloved responds with an invitation to "go out . . . into the vineyards, and see whether the vines have budded.")

Guidance from the Apostle Paul

Paul, in his often-quoted words about sexual behavior, is doing the same work as Mosaic law. He is thinking about sexuality in the context of the order of creation. In other words, Paul may be tweaking the specifics of Mosaic law, but in the grand scheme, he is not innovating. He is, like the leaders of the Old Testament, articulating boundaries and regulations that protect God's original intent that sex be expressed in marriage. . . .

Paul sometimes gets a reputation as a killjoy, a first-century prude who's concerned above all else with regulating people's sexual behavior. Abstracted from his larger vision of helping people live into God's ideals for creation, Paul's vision of human sexuality does indeed seem like a list of arbitrary rules. But Paul is not writing in a vacuum. He uses the literary technique of repetition to direct the reader's attention back to Genesis. In the middle of his first letter to the Corinthians, right after enjoining the Corinthians not to sleep with prostitutes and right before instructing the unmarried that it is better to marry than to burn, Paul quotes Genesis 2:24: "The two shall become one flesh." Paul's quotation is something of shorthand—it tells the reader to flip back to the second chapter of Genesis to find both the basis for and the elaboration of Paul's words on sexuality. . . .

This is not just a lesson in reading. It is also a pastoral point. Consider, as an example, the recent experience of my friend Kara, a campus minister in Illinois. Recently a student came to her, on fire for the Lord, and said, "I want to follow and serve Jesus, and the one thing I really want to know is, how far can I go with my boyfriend?" One could, I suppose, answer that question simply by pointing to a few verses from Paul, but a more complete, and perhaps more compelling, instruction is to begin with the picture of intended reality that is laid out in Genesis. Kara realized that answering her student's question required first answering a host of larger questions: *Who created us, and for what ends? What is God's creational intent?* and *What are we made for?*

I'll hazard a guess about Kara's student. When she's sitting on the sofa in a dark den with her boyfriend, random verses from Paul may not do much work. However, if this student's community helps form in her an understanding that she is God's creature, made for God's best purposes, she may indeed think very differently—even righteously—about sex, and bodies, and the context in which those bodies are to touch and be touched.

God and Creational Law

Our bodies and how we inhabit them point to the order of creation. God made us for sex within marriage; this is what the Reformed tradition would call a creational law. To see the biblical witness as an attempt to direct us to the created order, to God's rule of creation, is not to appeal to self-interest in a therapeutic or false way. It is rather to recognize the true goodness of God's creation; things as they were in the Garden of Eden are things at their most nourishing, they are things as they are meant to be. This is what Paul is saying when he speaks to the Corinthians: *Don't you know that when you give your body to a prostitute, you are uniting yourself to her?* To ask that question is to speak the wisdom of Proverbs in the idiom of law. It is a law that invites us into the created order of marital sex; a law that rightly orders our created desires for sexual pleasure and sexual connectedness; a law, in short, that cares for us and protects us, written by a Lawgiver who understands that life outside of God's created intent destroys us. By contrast, life lived inside the contours of God's law humanizes us and makes us beautiful. It makes us creatures living well in the created order. It gives us the opportunity to become who we are meant to be.

> *"Americans are forging a new sexual ethic for themselves. In typical American fashion, this new development is neither ideologically nor theologically driven. It is a response based on practicality and the civil guarantees of rights and liberties that most now just take for granted."*

Sex Is Morally Permissible Outside Traditional Marriage

Balfour Brickner

Some religious leaders and people of faith believe that sexual activity outside traditional marriage can be spiritually fulfilling, and they argue that religious restrictions on adult sexual activity outside marriage are unrealistic and prudish given the ways in which American culture and society have changed over the past few decades. The following viewpoint, written by Balfour Brickner, the senior rabbi emeritus at the Stephen Wise Free Synagogue in New York City, reflects this belief that a healthier "sexual ethic" is emerging in the United States.

As you read, consider the following questions:

1. What is the author's opinion of conservative religious organizations such as Focus on the Family, Concerned Women of America, and the Family Research Council?

2. How does the author feel about television shows such as *Sex and the City* that have considerable sexual content?

3. Who does the author compare to Constantine's legionnaires, who "carried [Christianity] to the world on . . . spear points"?

It is a truth that most of us know.

Politicians avoid discussing it publicly lest when they do they sound less honest than usual. The American population is pitifully hypocritical with it. Clergy, seeing it, offer neither wisdom, guidance nor leadership. Against it, the religious right conducts a fearsome but losing battle, while the broad extent of it is revealed by the mushrooming rash of gay marriages now flooding court houses across America.

What is this truth?

The nuclear family as we once knew it has crumbled. In its place a new understanding of family is emerging. That mythic television family of yesteryear, the happily married monogamous wife and husband, two drug-free children and a dog, living in a three-bedroom, two-bath house on a 100' x 100' plot in a cookie-cutter suburban development somewhere, hardly exists anywhere anymore. In fact, the reality is radically different.

Modern Trends

The most recent US census reveals that the marriage rate is declining precipitously, only 24 percent of households are made up of a married couple and children, and in some age cohorts as many as half of all marriages will end up in divorce. More people than ever before live together in permanent relationships without legal sanction. The number of unmarried couple households rose from 500,000 in 1970 to 5 million in 2004. More children are being born to or adopted—without social or religious stigma—by couples in such arrangements. It is almost the norm for gay and straight couples to live together unmarried and more widowed or divorced older folk find new partners and cohabit without marriage. A veritable epidemic of gay marriages has erupted across the land creating gay families that raise children in familial settings where, much to the dismay of braying religious fundamentalists, the kids are doing just fine with two mommies or two daddies. According to the 2000 census, 594,000 households in the United States were headed by same-sex partners, a figure considered by some experts to be conservative. Of those, about 33 percent of lesbian couples reported having children aged 18 or under, while 22 percent of male couples did.

Even the opprobrium of adultery has lost its moral and legal sting. In most of our nation's courts, adultery is no longer used as grounds for divorce. Its practice is so common that most of us just shrug on learning that our friends, neighbors or business associates are, or have been, involved in some "affair." After all, everyone knows that adulterous relationships are conducted regularly in the highest of professional, governmental and even clerical circles. So what?

The Conservative Viewpoint

Conservatives and religious fundamentalists represented by organizations like Focus on the Family, Concerned Women of America and the Family Research Council see these patterns as catastrophic, and do all in their power to reverse the trend. One can understand their desperation. After all, science, technology, philosophy, even Biblical studies, enlightened as they continue to be by archeology, have shattered their world at every level. They would like to see things return to some status quo ante where their world was secure, when folks believed the sun revolved around the earth, when there was no Hubble telescope to penetrate space to tell us that indeed our cosmos is 14 billion years old, not one created in six days, or when we could not prove that life evolved from lower to higher forms of being. The present situation, certainly the teaching of evolution in the schools, and the exposure of the young to "humanistic ideas," challenges the credibility of their faith at every level.

Bruised by these changes, angered by the hostility of what became a largely post-Christian era, many, mostly Christian traditionalists at first, sought solace by retreating into an otherworldly version of an earlier Christian identity. This movement became the fundamentalist stream of American Christianity that today [2004] dominates our nation's political life. They are frightened by, and infuriated with, contemporary social behavior, especially America's changed sexual attitudes and practices. While forgiving their own religious leaders their highly publicized sexual excesses, they cannot tolerate what they believe the rest of us are up to. They see such behavior as hastening the decline, if not the destruction, of all social structures. Little wonder they rail so vehemently against what they consider libertine sexual behavior among adolescents as well as between unmarried adults. To them, the use of, or teaching of birth control, family planning, a woman's right to abortion, etc. merely spreads the contagion. Such behavior, they are convinced, hastens the end of civilization.

But, since world catastrophe [the apocalypse] is a part of their theology anyway, one wonders why the deterioration of the family should worry them so much. Since in their view it is speeding the coming of the end of life as we know it, and the end is to be welcomed as a necessary precursor to the great Parousia [second coming of Jesus Christ] and subsequent rapture upwards into the heavenly future, why not welcome the destruction of the family brought on, as they claim, by libertines, liberals, humanists, "eastern elites" and other troubling types? Instead of cursing us as a form of the devil incarnate, (which they do) they should welcome us as doing their God's work. They don't. Perhaps there is an unresolved lacunae [gap] in their theological system?

A New Sexual Ethic

For those of us whose sociological views are not shaped by either religious or secular fundamentalism, America's changes in sexual attitudes and behavior do not represent a cataclysmic decline in morality. They do mean that our society is beginning to understand, accept and express sex and sexuality in more honest terms, stripped of the hypocrisy which characterized so much of our past behavior. We no longer see the need to decry sex publicly, while privately gorging ourselves on it. It means we are beginning to give a totally new definition to the word "family," one that is not dependent on a legal sanction, even as we recognize that the ideals conveyed by words like "love," "commitment" and "responsibility" continue to hold as much psychological power as any legal document ever did. People still want and seek family and all it ideally represents, including a home—that secure anchoring place which [American poet] Robert Frost once described as the place where, when you go there, they have to take you in.

Americans are forging a new sexual ethic for themselves. In typical American fashion, this new development is neither ideologically nor theologically driven. It is a response based on practicality and the civil guarantees of rights and liberties which most now just take for granted. Rarely do I officiate at a wedding nowadays where the bride and groom have separate addresses prior to the ceremony. Working couples find it too expensive to live separately. Older couples cohabit without the benefit of marriage for many reasons, some quite practical: threatened loss of Social Security for one of the two, disrupt-

"SOMEWHERE LIKE SODOM AND GOMORRAH, BUT WITHOUT THE GUILT!"

"Somewhere like Sodom and Gomorrah, but without the guilt!" cartoon by Dan Rosandich. CartoonStock.com.

ing inheritance arrangements for family members. The reasons are legion and legitimate.

Modern Women and Sexual Ethics

Most women now work. Their economic and social independence is handmaid to their freedom. Sexual freedom, greatly strengthened by the easy availability of effective birth control, is an undisputed corollary of their won and civilly protected status. This does not signal licentiousness or a casting off of personal behavioral standards. It is a long-delayed equity and women rightfully demand that the world see, understand and respect complete female emancipation at all levels of life.

This new status is remarkable for its honesty, its candor, its explicit demand for equal sexual pleasure and for its ability to take sex seriously while viewing it with a certain knowing humor and openness. Ours is the age of "Cosmo culture" where in the pages of that magazine [*Cosmopolitan*] one can read of various techniques women can employ to bring them and their partners to simultaneously shared moments of exquisite physical pleasure. The mechanics of sex are taught openly, in print, on television, easily available for all to learn. Hopefully when that is achieved, the next step, understanding the mystique of sexuality, will be fully developed and enjoyed. We have turned a corner in our attitude toward human sexuality. *Playboy*, Larry Flynt [publisher of *Hustler*] and the comedian Lenny Bruce may have seemed outrageous in their time, but it took their excesses and the challenges they provoked in our courts to shatter the Comstockian [after Anthony Comstock, U.S. Postal Inspector known for censoring material] and puritanical restrictions that inhibited our culture's progress. People need to feel good—not guilty—about their sexuality and the new sexual age in which we are living. Publications like *Cosmopolitan*, TV shows like "Sex and the City" and "The L Word" and some of our more creative writers for film and stage are taking us there. But in all of this, one major social structure seems to be missing: America's religious institutions. The instrument that is supposed to give us our spiritual and moral base is absent. It is fair to ask: Are our religious establishments part of the problem or part of the solution?

The Question of Gay Clergy

The Methodist church's conflict over whether or not to allow "outed" lesbians to serve as clergy and the Episcopal church's response to the consecration as bishop of an openly gay priest are moments of light in an otherwise "wine dark" religious sea. In both of these instances, those who prevailed fought for the right of their clergy to serve. If only they were not noteworthy moments because of their uniqueness. It is depressing to see institutions that profess to see God's spirit in everyone allow their slavish adherence to archaic, doctrinal dogma drive people from one another and from some God they teach as the ultimate exemplar of love and understanding. A decade from now they will look back on this struggle and feel shame and humiliating embarrassment. They will wonder how we let such bigoted ignorance out of its cell.

Those in the Methodist communion who would have denied ordination to a professed lesbian minister, and the substantial minority within the American Episcopal church and its worldwide Anglican communion who oppose the consecration of a gay bishop base their opposition to accepting their clergy's homosexuality on a text found in the Hebrew Bible where in the 22nd verse of the 18th chapter of the book of Leviticus it states: "You shall not lie with a male as with a woman; it is an abomination."

Amazing that they choose to be governed by this demand, and risk splitting their already-weakened churches, while failing totally to observe the command in Deuteronomy 24 to stone all adulterers. Perhaps they fear too great a diminishment of their ranks were they too closely to observe that commandment? Moreover, one cannot help observing that the same texts which condemn homosexuality also condemn the eating of shellfish, yet nowadays it is hard to find a conservative churchman campaigning against the eating of shrimp, half a dozen oysters on the half shell or a boiled lobster. The faithful do have a tendency to conveniently pick and choose their commandments, don't they? Even more amazing is the realization that no such condemnation of homosexuality can be found in the basic four gospels of the New Testament, the texts most Christians, and certainly traditionalists, elevate to a position of authority transcending that of the Hebrew Bible, which they believe the New Testament supercedes.

Rejection Without Biblical Merit

An exclusion of homosexuals from all aspects of church life, including the highest calling of priestly leadership, cannot be validated from the four gospels or from the Hebrew Bible. One rabbinic scholar wisely reminds us that the Torah teaches that every human being is created in the image of divinity. Its entire leitmotif [recurring theme] is one that urges compassion and empathy for the stranger in our midst, reminding us that Jews were once oppressed strangers in the land of Egypt and from that experience should know the heart of the stranger (the torture of alienation to which they are subjected). The Hebrew Bible is full of sex and it is always presented in positive terms.

"Let your fountain be blessed, and rejoice in the wife of your youth, a lovely deer, a graceful doe. May her breasts satisfy you all times, may you be intoxicated always by her love" Proverbs 5:18–19. If that doesn't persuade you, turn to The Song of Songs 7:6–9.

This major thrust of biblical intent certainly trumps any single statement any where in scripture that might condemn homosexual behavior as "an abomination." Moreover, if it is true that *all* (italics mine) humans are created in the divine image, do not those who oppose granting gays their full rights negate the truth of biblical sentiment by urging us to treat gays differently from others? Or would they argue that gays are not either fully human or fully divine? Medical science would testify that they are fully human, albeit perhaps created with a different genetic arrangement—and doesn't that in some ways describe all of us? As to full divinity? One wonders what special gifts are possessed by opponents of full rights for homosexuals that enable them to discern the nature and the will of divinity.

Why are all but the right wing religious institutions so impotent in this arena. It cannot be because their bible teaches that sexuality is some negative, terrible hurtful business. No text in the four synoptic gospels deals negatively with sex. Other New Testament materials such as Romans and Corinthians may, but they are of a different qualitative category. So why the silence? Is it because those who speak for the church feel they have nothing to say? Is it because their clergy leadership is afraid of polarizing the membership of their institution at a time when those memberships are becoming increasingly conservative?

In the 1960s and 1970s organized religion played a critical role in the civil rights struggle, and later in the antiwar movement. Today it seems to have either failed to understand the seriousness of America's sexual revolution or it has turned away from its historic prophetic mandate. For whatever reasons, our religious bodies are not part of the solution to America's struggle to achieve full sexual freedom for all of its citizens.

Gay Rights and Christianity

Historians tell us that Christianity was carried to the world on the spear points of Constantine's legionnaires. Without that compelling persuasive force, Christianity might have languished for centuries as just another cult or faith in the ancient world, competing with all others for people's hearts and minds. Today [2004], the new battle is for full sexual freedom. It is being carried forward by a most unlikely band of foot soldiers: gays demanding their civil rights. Less than a decade ago, gays legitimately feared that in many parts of this country public exposure might cost them their lives. They no longer fear public opinion. They are demanding that the social and civil engines of our society confirm the rights they correctly believe are theirs by constitutional guarantee. Anger has replaced fear. Organized massive presence has replaced closeted isolation and the population of this vast country is slowly being forced to understand and accept the legitimacy of their demands. The trend toward total acceptance of homosexuality is irreversibly underway in America. It may take longer in some areas of our country than in others but the outcome is inevitable. No one could have foreseen the speed with which this has all happened. Perhaps it took the crucifixion of a gay young man [Matthew Shepard, murdered in 1998] on the barbed wire of a rural fence in Wyoming to further the goal. Perhaps it was the bludgeoning to death of a gay soldier [Barry Winchell, murdered in 1999] in a US Army barracks that helped attitudes change. Possibly it was gays demanding the right to march under their own banner in a St. Patrick's Day parade, or their own Gay Pride Week marches that helped change people's attitudes.

Probably it was a cumulation of all such incidents, each somewhat minuscule, but combined they became an irresistible force, given even greater focus by a president's pandering effort to define who is eligible for civil marriage by proposing to amend the US Constitution. [George W. Bush urged in 2004 an amendment defining marriage solely as the union between a man and a woman.] This action, initiated in an election year to mollify [soothe] a right-wing constituency on which the present administration heavily depends for electoral and financial support, has done more to galvanize the gay community and those who support it than perhaps any other single event since the 1980 shooting attack by a disgruntled former police officer at the Ramrod, a New York City gay bar.

Confronting Hypocrisies

We are slowly coming to terms with our own hypocrisies. Whereas in 1991, 71 percent of Americans said gay sex was always wrong, by 2002 that number had fallen to 53 percent with 32 percent saying that gay sex was not wrong at all. It is when the word "marriage" is introduced into the equation that toleration levels decline. For some reason(s) our citizenry, while increasingly supportive of extending legal rights to gays and their partners, including same-sex unions, balk when the issue of marriage is raised. Marriage, at least as a paradigm, seems to be the one issue about which Americans continue to care deeply. Allowing marriage for gays somehow seems to attack those religious foundations of our lives we would like to uphold in an ideal world, even though most do little to give them practical expression in their daily behavior. There is an element of hypocrisy here, but it is alright. We need occasionally to grant ourselves our slight idiosyncrasies. No society can be expected always to measure up to the plumb line of strict consistency on all social matters. Other societies may be more honest in their approach to sanctifying gay coupling. We, however, are still a young, somewhat adolescent society, struggling to emerge from the influence of Calvinist orthodoxies. Perhaps the debate over gay marriage should not be fought on religious grounds, but it is. While we seem able to tolerate gay civil unions, marriage strikes at the heart of approval. It is easier to tolerate than it is to approve. And the prospect of gay marriage threatens people with a government stamp of approval on homosexuality. Americans are not yet ready to go that far.

One psychoanalyst, Dr. Peter Wolson observed:

> The prospect of gay marriage ... strikes at the traditional nuclear anchor of American life and powerful childhood forces, it challenges the basic black and white stereotypes we grew up with and once that black and white is challenged, it brings us all into this crazy zone of existential uncertainty. (*New York Times*, August 10, 2003)

What is existentially threatening today will soon become non-threatening reality. We learned to accept integration. We have learned to live with adultery, and with couples living together extramaritally. We have even learned to accept female equality. We will soon get used to the idea of gay marriage.

Sex has changed in America. There is no going back.

"When it comes to sexual morality, many of us revel in relativism, also known as 'tolerance.' We no longer hide the fact that we live together and love together outside of marriage or that we have a sexual relationship with a person of the same sex."

Attitudes About Sexuality Have Become Healthier Since the 1960s

Don Lattin

This viewpoint asserts that American sexual ethics have improved and attitudes toward sexuality have become healthier since the 1960s, when the "sexual revolution" first emerged. According to author Don Lattin, who was religion writer for the San Francisco Chronicle *for two decades, evolving ideas about sexual morality and ethics have made many Americans happier and more spiritually fulfilled. He acknowledges that sexual activity that takes place outside some ethical boundaries is immoral, but he argues that conservative religious conceptions of sexual ethics and morality are deeply flawed and should be dismissed.*

As you read, consider the following questions:

1. Who does the author refer to as "cafeteria Catholics"?

2. What is the author's perspective on the 1950s and its alleged emphasis on "traditional family values"?

3. How does Lattin use the life and teachings of Jesus to support his arguments about sexual morality?

For the past few years, I've talked to lots of "unchurched" Gen Xers and their Baby Boomer parents for a new book titled *Following Our Bliss—How the Spiritual Ideals of the Sixties Shape Our Lives Today*. Among the questions we explore are how one lives an ethical life outside the Judeo-Christian mainstream. What are your guideposts if you don't want your rules etched in stone and placed in the Supreme Court building in Montgomery, Ala.? [reference to Alabama Chief Justice Roy Moore's display of Ten Commandments in state building; monument removed, 2003] How do former fundamentalists decide what is right or wrong if they no longer fear God nor follow all 10 of the Ten Commandments? How do lapsed Catholics make moral decisions about sexuality without turning to the catechism of the Roman Catholic Church?

"The motivation for living an ethical life is not just intellectual or someone frightening you. It can be based emotionally on your sense of compassion and empathy. That's where soul and spirit come together," said Thomas Moore, a free-thinking Catholic and author of *Care of the Soul*, one of the mega-selling spirituality books of the 1990s.

"That's very important in an ethical life. You realize that we're all in this together. We live in a diverse world and need to have empathy for people with diverse views and lifestyles. The church has tried to use fear, but it doesn't work."

Moore and I were talking about how people can be Catholic without obeying the edicts of the pope or their Catholic bishop. Back in the 1950s, when he was entering adolescence, Moore left home to begin the years of study required for ordination as a Roman Catholic priest in a religious order. Thirteen years later, just six months before he was to take his final vows, Moore opted out of the clerical life. It was 1967, and Moore was 26.

Today [2003], Thomas Moore, writer, has influenced far more American Catholics than he would have as Thomas Moore, priest. "I'm still a monk at heart and the writing of these books is my spiritual practice," said Moore, who has two children. "It's not just a job. I realize how much of my Catholicism is involved in my life, but it's not the Catholicism that the church advocates. I don't care if I follow all the rules, but I have the spirit of it. In my own way, I do practice the faith. My Catholicism is part of my nature. It's part of me. It's a cultural thing and it makes no sense to me to disown it. So the alternative is to redefine it."

Spiritual seekers of my generation—those of us who profess to be into "spirituality, but not religion"—are notorious for this personalized approach to finding faith and making moral decisions. If we are Catholic, we are "cafeteria Catholics," picking and choosing our spiritual and ethical nourishment from the Roman menu. We stand accused of moral relativism in our ethics and philosophy—believing that right and wrong and good and bad change with time and circumstance.

Not that long ago, sex between two men or two women was considered immoral, unnatural or at least unspeakable by the civic and spiritual establishment. Today, we have openly gay members of Congress, the Board of Supervisors and the Episcopal House of Bishops.

When it comes to sexual morality, many of us revel in relativism, also known as "tolerance." We no longer hide the fact that we live together and love together outside of marriage, or that we have a sexual relationship with a person of the same sex.

Since the sexual revolution of the '60s and '70s, Jewish and Christian denominations have struggled with the culture's conflicting concepts of sexual morality. And the debate shows no signs of abating. Earlier this year, conservatives in the worldwide Anglican communion threatened schism when the Episcopal bishops of the United States ordained an openly gay bishop. That was just weeks after the Vatican declared that civil recognition of gay unions was a "legalization of evil." At their big summer church conventions, mainline Protestant denominations like the Presbyterian Church USA argue about gay rights and morality of homosexual unions on an annual basis.

Meanwhile, millions of younger Americans—the ones who are actually having most of the sex—could care less what Episcopal bishops, Vatican officials or Presbyterian delegates think about all this. But that does not mean their sexuality isn't connected to their spirituality or their sense of right and wrong. . . .

Rebecca Ann Parker is an ordained Methodist minister and president of Starr King School of Ministry, a Unitarian-Universalist seminary and member of the Graduate Theological Union consortium on Berkeley's "Holy Hill."

We're sitting in her office talking about sex. She is a short woman, with an easy smile and gray hair cut in a short and simple style. Parker and I were both born in 1953, smack dab in the middle of the Baby Boom years, and we both came of age in the middle of the sexual revolution.

"I was just coming of age in the early 1970s and remember the sexual freedom of the time. There was a sense that old boundaries were oppressive and destroying the life spirit. In a lot of ways that was true. The old boundaries were not healthy, but not having any values was also unhealthy. It wasn't that good for women, it wasn't that good for children, and maybe it wasn't that good for men either.

"In the last 30 years [between 1970 and 2000] we've been reconstructing an understanding of right relationship, or ethical boundaries," she said. "You had the women's movement

Sexuality and Sacredness

Historically, the Catholic church has laid down sexual laws that reflect a certain imperial attitude: Have as many children as possible in order to spread Catholicism far and wide. Protestant teaching emphasized that sex should be dour, painful, and an assigned duty of marriage. It was definitely not something one talked about. As Christians we have a lot of bad history to overcome. Maybe we should add "sex is good, sex is holy" to our daily prayers. . . .

Too much of the church's teaching on sex has been about rules and regulations. That approach won't work any more. Read the story of Jacob and Laban in Genesis. Jacob starts out as a "righteous man"—a rule-follower—but in his 20 years of sexual intrigue with Laban over Rachel and Leah, Jacob breaks all the rules. It is in this crucible of sin, however, that God transforms Jacob into a "baal teshuva"—a man of mercy.

This is what God intends—a life-shaping narrative that allows sex, sexuality, and sensuality to be part of the sacred and complex interplay of light and shadow across the human heart. In recovering a sacred, respectful sexuality we make our bodies a fit dwelling place for God. It may not get as much press as sin, but it's a good definition of church.

Rose Marie Berger, "Managing the Erotic Life,"
Sojourners, vol. 31, no. 3, May–June 2002.

deeply divided over pornography, or S&M [sadomasochism-gaining sexual pleasure by inflicting pain on another person]. OK. Let's say 'Sex is good' rather than 'Sex is bad.' I'm for that. But that kind of either/or is not an adequate way of parsing the problem. It's more complex than that. Even when you say sexuality is good, you have to ask 'When is it good?' Sex is this wonderful thing, but it's a little like fire. It can warm you, or it can burn you."

Then I asked Parker about sexual ethics—about the widespread disagreement in America today about what kind of sex is "good" and what kind of sex is "bad." What's the connection between our attitudes about monogamy, homosexuality and our religious tradition?

"There is a connection between monotheism and monogamy. Being faithful to the one true God. You have images of idolatry and apostasy being articulated as adultery or sexual licentiousness. Your right relationship to God is monogamous. You have one God like you have no other loves. Then you've got the notion of God creating male and female to be right with God. Those are the orders of creation. So to follow God's orders is to be heterosexual. Actually, the Bible itself has many more complicated human sexual behaviors than that. But for those of us born in the '50s, the ethics of that era were monogamous heterosexuality was right, and sex outside of marriage was wrong. If you were a Catholic, you also had the idea that sex for pleasure was wrong. What evolved from the 1950s was the idea that, 'Well, maybe sexuality is good.' Then the idea that sexual diversity was good."

OK. So far, so good. But on what do you base a sexual ethic if you don't base it on God, the Bible or religious tradition?

"I would base it on what's good for children," Parker replied. "I think it's good for children to have adults who are committed to them without question."

It's hard to argue against parents being totally committed to their children—but here goes:

Today, the family has been raised up as the most sacred and sovereign unit of society. Many of the families profiled in "Following Our Bliss" paid less attention to the kids than the children wanted, but the neglect was mostly benign, the byproduct of social idealism or a life a bit too centered on self-improvement. One of the themes running through my interviews with people born into the spiritual counterculture of the '60s was this feeling that their parents were not there for them. It didn't matter that they were worshiping strange gods, following some messianic prophet or living promiscuous lives. It wasn't that Mom and Dad were out saving the world, or spreading Krishna consciousness, but simply that they were not available to the family. Many of these parents were more concerned about changing the world than raising their families.

Looking back on it, many of these adult children of the '60s retain some resentment about not being the center of their parents' universe. But those who inherited Mom and Dad's social idealism also see that there was a lot in the world that needed to be changed, and there still is. . . .

Sixties-bashing is facile [easy, simplistic]. In the 1990s, those titillating times were subject to endless sniping by the talking heads of television, apostles of the ordinary and other neo-conservative pundits [experts]. For many Christian commentators, the '60s became a metaphor for the Fall From Grace. It was more convenient to blame drug addiction, poverty, teen pregnancy and the breakdown of the family on a past period of permissiveness. It was also a good political strategy. Criticizing the excesses of the '60s shifts attention away from the recent undoing of the vital social gains of the decade. It was easier to preach a narrow and regressive sexual morality than to look at other forces threatening poor and middle-class families in the late 20th century—like the desperate shortage of affordable housing and the grinding necessity for both parents to hold jobs.

Our appraisal of the '60s flows from our ideas about the '50s—and many of those ideas are wrong. Sixties bashers claim America's moral, religious and familial life reached shining heights in the '50s, then collapsed into a cacophony of selfishness and sin. America's "Greatest Generation," we are told, saved the world in the '40s, then moved to the suburbs and set us on the path of peace and prosperity. In this fantasy, all began to unravel in the '60s, when a rebellious generation tore society apart and couldn't put it back together again. Our most grievous loss was said to be "traditional family values," three words that became the political battle cry of reactionary, post-'60s politics and religion.

In reality, there wasn't much about the faith and families of the '50s that were "traditional." If anything, the '50s was the aberrant decade, not the '60s and '70s. The post-World War II era saw an abnormal emphasis on piety, patriotism and the nuclear family. In fact, the decade was just a blip on the long-term charts of public piety. Our religious "revival" had more to do with demographics and politics than the hand of God. The Baby Boomers reached their Sunday-school years. This is when many families traditionally—and often temporarily—reconnect with church or synagogue.

Enough about "the greatest generation." It had its greatness, to be sure, but it is also the generation that built Japanese internment camps, saluted McCarthyism and mostly turned its face away from racism and anti-Semitism. Many of the problems we blame on the '60s—child abuse, domestic violence, substance abuse—were no less prevalent in the '50s. We just didn't talk about it then. It was much easier to hide all that behind the walls of our now-separate homes out in the suburbs. . . .

Powerful spirits moved the religious revolution of the '60s: idealism, innovation, empowerment and the search for authentic experience. They remain the hallmarks of the era. There was a thirst for authenticity, for telling it like it is. There was a turning away from materialism, greed and old roles. Many of us replayed Dustin Hoffman's role in the 1967 film "The Graduate," searching for our own life and our own set of values. Benjamin was right. You don't have to go into plastics. You can follow your bliss. There was a feeling of hope in the '60s that's hard for young people to imagine today.

Yet conservative evangelicals look at the signs of the times in San Francisco and tell us all signs point straight to hell. We are the mecca of alternative lifestyles, and as the Bay Area goes, so goes the nation. Take, for example, the following paragraph from a recent book by sociologist Alan Wolfe called *Moral Freedom: The Search for Virtue in a World of Choice.* Wolfe surveys the populations in places like Tipton, Iowa, and San Antonio, Texas, and comes to San Francisco only to find the counterpoint to all that is right and true in America.

"The most notorious events of the dreaded 1960s—the Free Speech Movement, violent resistance against the military draft, the rise of the Black Panthers, and the drug and music scene with its ground zero at Haight-Ashbury—happened either in San Francisco or across the bay in Berkeley and Oakland," Wolfe writes. "In the next decade Castro Street would become the main street of gay America, not only a direct confrontation with traditional American morality but also, by the end of the 1970s, a disease that seemed to vindicate the wrath of God. With a climate and scenic beauty too good to be true, San Francisco came to represent a repudiation of the self-discipline and delayed gratification that once constituted the core of both capitalist and Christian virtue. Political and theological conservatives therefore find in San Francisco everything that goes wrong when people believe that they can somehow live without obedience to firm rules of moral authority, handed down by tradition, tested by centuries of experience, and inscribed in the great moral and religious texts of the West."

And you thought we were just having a good time.

Don't get me wrong. Being a child of the '60s was not easy. Divorce is hard on families, and from 1960 to the mid-1980s, the divorce rate tripled and the number of children in one-parent homes doubled. Meanwhile, the percentage of teenage mothers who were unwed jumped from 15 percent to 61 percent. None of those are healthy trends, but it's too easy to blame the bogeymen of the counterculture and '60s permissiveness. Most people who divorce remarry and form new and extended kinship networks. Back in the '50s, pregnant girls got married, but they produced a lot of unhappy marriages and unloved children. Bad marriages are not necessarily better than good single-parent homes.

The leaders of today's Christian Right [in 2003] respond to the 1960s and women's liberation with fire-and-brimstone rhetoric. Pat Robertson, the televangelist and former GOP presidential candidate, proclaimed in a fund-raising letter in the 1990s that feminism was inspiring women to "leave their husbands, kill their children, practice witchcraft, destroy capitalism and become lesbians."

It's hard to decide which part of Robertson's rant is most shocking, especially from a man who claims to be a follower of Jesus, but let's just consider the parts about leaving husbands and destroying capitalism. According to the Bible, Jesus said his true disciple must reject his earthly life to follow the Master—he must "hate his own father and mother and wife and children and brothers and sisters." As for capitalism, the Savior advises the rich man to "sell what you own, and give the money to the poor, and you will have treasure in heaven; then come follow me." So much for capitalism and family values.

So what would Jesus do? What would he find good and bad about the spiritual legacy of the '60s? Search the Bible for clues about the Savior's worries about sex, wine and celebration, and you won't find much. And the Nazarene does not appear to have been a great advocate of traditional religion or traditional families. He inveighed against the accumulation of wealth and talked instead about voluntary simplicity, peace, justice, love and communal living. He was much more interested in saving the world than raising a family. Sound familiar?

Then, and now, we need to watch out for those who use sexual morality and "traditional family values" as smoke screens for selfishness. Sexual ethics and family values are important, but no more important than social ethics. It's time for us to stop buying into the reaction against San Francisco and the '60s, and find our way back to what was best about that time and this place.

"Since [the 1960s] sexual freedom has proliferated, to the point where many people treat sexual conduct as though it were outside the scope of moral judgment altogether."

Attitudes About Sexuality Have Worsened Since the 1960s

Roger Scruton

Modern Americans have redefined sexual morality so that they can indulge in selfish and destructive sexual behavior without guilt, claims Roger Scruton in the following viewpoint. He believes that this practice first emerged in the 1960s and that it now looms as a serious threat to traditional marriage, upon which rests "the future of society." Roger Scruton is a British businessman, publisher, composer, and author whose credits include more than 30 books, including novels and works on philosophy and on political and cultural commentary.

As you read, consider the following questions:

1. According to the author, what is the fundamental difference between erotic and pornographic materials?

Roger Scruton, "The Moral Birds and Bees: Sex and Marriage, Properly Understood," *National Review*, vol. 55, September 15, 2003. Copyright © 2003 by National Review, Inc., 215 Lexington Avenue, New York, NY 10016. Reproduced by permission.-

2. What is Scruton's perspective on the issue of gay marriage?

3. According to Scruton, how have Americans avoided charges that they are hypocrites when it comes to issues of sexual behavior and morality?

In the England of the Forties, when my parents were courting, terms like "moral," "decent," and "clean living" applied primarily to sexual behavior. Immorality meant sleeping around (and how innocent the word "sleeping" now sounds!); indecency meant unsolicited advances; dirtiness meant whatever put the sexual object before the loving subject. Sexual morality issued from two firm and seemingly immovable premises: that the sexual act is innocent only when sanctified by marriage, and that marriage is a commitment between man and woman, to share their life, fortunes, and family, for better and for worse, until death do them part.

The Sixties put paid to that vision. Since then sexual freedom has proliferated, to the point where many people treat sexual conduct as though it were outside the scope of moral judgment altogether. It really doesn't matter, it is often said, what people do together, provided they freely enjoy it. Sure, pedophilia is wrong. But that is because real consent requires maturity; anything that adults agree to do in private is morally unimpeachable.

Now you can take that line and still believe in marriage, as a uniquely valuable institution with a distinctive place in the scheme of things. You may recognize that children need families, and that families depend on marriage as their binding principle. You may recognize this, and still believe that there is nothing wrong with extra-marital affairs, or intra-marital promiscuity (i.e., orgies, swapping). However, you would also have to believe that marital love can endure without sexual fidelity, that jealousy can be refined away from sexual love and eventually discarded, that marriages can dispense with the

Sex Always Affects Relationships

Our culture tells us that sex need not be taken seriously. A man has an affair and says, "It's nothing personal. It was just sex." College kids practice "hooking up" and say, "It's no big deal. It's just sex." People immerse themselves in pornography and visit strip clubs and say, "Hey, no one was harmed. It's entertainment." The truth is, there is no such thing as sex in a vacuum. Sex always affects relationships, it always affects you, and it always affects your mate. When sexual release is pursued outside of the one-man-one-woman sexual celebration of marriage, then the sacredness of sex is violated. The very heart of this holy union is broken. Sex always has tremendous consequences, either for incredible good or devastating harm.

Tim A. Gardner, "Sex's Mission: Why God Created Sexual Boundaries," Marriage Partnership, *vol. 19, issue 2, Summer 2002.*

kind of existential commitment whereby husband and wife consecrate their lives to each other. You would have to believe that sexual pleasure can be treated as an adjunct to our personal emotions, something that can be tasted in any circumstances and regardless of moral and personal ties. In short you would have to believe that human beings are quite different from those creatures described in our art and literature, for whom sexual desire has taken the form of erotic love and in whom erotic love has generally aspired to marriage.

Discarding Considerations of Sexual Morality

Many people do believe all that. Persuaded by the "research" reports of the Kinsey Institute, by Margaret Mead's fabricated account of sex in Samoa, by the Reich-Fromm-Norman O. Brown liberationist orthodoxy, and by latter-day antinomians [believers that faith alone can bring salvation] like Michel Foucault, they have come to assume that the attempts to distinguish right from wrong in sexual conduct, to separate legitimate from illegitimate sexual relations, and to surround the sexual act itself with an ethic of "pollution and taboo" (as the early anthropologists described it) are both unnecessary and oppressive. The only correct response to the problem posed by human sexuality, they believe, is to recognize that it is not a problem. It is we who choose, in Foucault's idiom to "problematize" the sexual act, and we do so in order to fortify hierarchical and oppressive relations that do us no conceivable good. By discarding sexual morality we free ourselves from our "mind forg'd manacles," [from English poet William Blake] so as to enjoy the harmless pleasures that the spoilsports have for so long taken pleasure in spoiling.

According to the gurus of sexual liberation, the real purpose of sex is not to express love or to generate children (which is another way of expressing love) but to obtain pleasurable sensations. Sexual initiation, according to their view of things, means learning to overcome guilt and shame, to put aside our hesitations, and to enjoy what is described in their literature (which is rapidly becoming the literature of "sex education" in our schools) as "good sex." This can occur with any partner of either sex, and requires no institutional preparation and no social endorsement.

That picture leaves out of consideration the phenomenon that distinguishes us from the other animals, and that also generates the need for a sexual morality, namely desire. Sexual desire is not a desire for sensations. It is a desire for a person: and I mean a person, not his or her body, conceived as an object in the physical world, but the person conceived as an incarnate subject, in whom the light of self-consciousness shines and who confronts me eye to eye and I to I. True desire is also a kind of petition: It demands reciprocity, mutuality, and a shared surrender. It is therefore compromising, jealous, and also threatening. No pursuit of a mere sensation could be compromising, jealous, or threatening in this way. Here lies the distinction between the erotic and the pornographic. Erotic literature is about wanting another person; pornography is about wanting sex.

The interpersonal nature of desire explains why unwanted advances are forbidden by the one to whom they might be addressed, and why they may be experienced as a kind of contamination. It explains why rape is so grave a crime: for rape is an invasion of the victim's freedom, and a dragging of the subject into the world of things. If you describe desire in the terms used by the advocates of liberation, the outrage and pollution of rape become impossible to explain. In fact, just about everything in human sexual behavior becomes impossible to explain. Which is why our society is now so confused about sex. We advocate a neutral, scientific view of sex, as a kind of pleasurable sensation in the private parts (which are rapidly ceasing to be private). And by teaching this view of things to children, we encourage them to a premature and depersonalized interest in their own sexuality. In effect we are endorsing in our heads a view of sex that we know in our hearts to be evil. For at some level we all recognize what our behavior denies, that true "sex education" consists not in permitting pleasure but in forbidding it, by fostering shame. And as our society loses its sense of shame, we begin to fear for our children, becoming hysterical at the thought of all those pedophiles out there—who are really the pedophiles in here, the very people who are eliciting in their children a depersonalized interest in sex.

Morality and Sexual Desire

Traditional morality did not exist to prevent sexual pleasure, but to assist in the growth of sexual desire, as an individualizing bond between people. Shame was the barrier behind which erotic energy accumulated, to the point where it could overflow as desire. Marriage was seen as the institutional expression of desire, rather than a way of restricting or denying it. The first purpose of marriage was to consecrate the union of the partners, to make holy and inviolable what would otherwise be a merely secular contract of cohabitation. Such was the view of marriage that arose in medieval Europe, and that is enshrined in our own literature of love. Nor have other civilizations really disagreed, despite all the varied customs that distinguish them. Islamic, Chinese, Japanese, and Hindu cultures have all concurred in representing sexual desire as an existential bond rather than a fleeting appetite, to be hedged round with shame and hesitation until socially endorsed and ceremonially accepted.

As with all moral sentiments, however, this one concerning the connection between desire and marriage has both a subjective meaning and a social role. Its subjective meaning lies in the exaltation and ennobling of our sexual urges, which are lifted from the realm of appetite and reconstituted as rational commitments. Its social role is to facilitate the sacrifices on which the next generation depends. Marriage is not merely a tie between man and woman; it is the principal forum in which social capital is passed on. By tying sexual fulfillment to the bearing of children, marriage offers a double guarantee of a stable home: the guarantee that comes from erotic love, and the guarantee that comes from the shared love of offspring. It offers children durable affection, a secure territory, moral examples, and moral discipline.

This is all so obvious as barely to deserve mention. As James Q. Wilson has shown, being born to an unmarried mother is by far the most significant factor disposing children to a life of crime—more significant than IQ, race, culture, or education. All of us therefore have a deep and lasting interest in marriage, as the only known way to reproduce the moral order. We have an interest in ensuring that this institution is not trivialized or abused, not reduced to a Disneyland caricature or deprived of its privileged place in the scheme of things—which is, socially speaking, that of a link between generations.

The Nature of Marriage

Marriage in a religious society is a religious event: not a contract between mortals but a vow before the gods. Such a marriage raises the bond between husband and wife from the secular to the sacred sphere, so that whoever breaks the bond commits an act of sacrilege. Civil marriage (as introduced in modern times by the French revolutionaries) has gradually displaced the religious institution, so that marriage is now conducted by the civil authorities, and the change in status is not ontological [concerning the nature of being], like the change from secular to sacred, but legal. In effect marriage has become a contract and has gradually assumed the provisional and temporary character of all merely secular arrangements. This was not the intention of those who invented civil marriage. In taking over and secularizing the institution of marriage the state was hoping to confer fiscal privileges and legal guarantees that would substitute for religious sanctions, and so help to make our commitments durable. It did this from the belief that marriage is vital to the future of society. The state in effect lent its aid to traditional sexual morality, by privileging faithful union between man and wife. And it did so for the very good reason that the future of society depends on this kind of union.

Now, however, the marriage contract is being enlarged to accommodate the permissive morality. Marriage is ceasing to be a sacrificial union of lovers, in which future generations have a stake, and becoming a transitory agreement between people living now. It is from this perspective that we should view the controversy over gay marriage.

This is not really a controversy about the rights, freedoms, and life-chances of homosexuals. It is a controversy about the institution of marriage itself. Can marriage retain its privileged place in our moral thinking when so effectively severed from the process of social reproduction? Already the secularization of marriage has led to easy divorce, serial polygamy, and growing insecurity among children. But marriage in its fundamental meaning is a form of lifelong commitment, in which absent generations have a stake. If marriage can be celebrated between homosexual partners, then it will cease entirely to be anything more than a contract of cohabitation, and the legal and fiscal privileges attached to it will seem both unjustified and dangerous, so many openings to litigation. Lovers' quarrels, exalted into marital disputes, will be endowed with an intransigent bitterness, while transient crushes will be foisted on friends and colleagues as institutional facts. In effect, marriage, as the institution through which society offers its endorsement and support to the raising of children, will have ceased to exist.

The demand to make institutions conform to our desires, rather than our desires to institutions, is one of the great American failings. Thanks to their Puritan heritage, Americans regard hypocrisy as a serious vice, and sin as so lamentable a condition that it must be avoided at all costs. If the only way to avoid sin is to redefine your sins as innocent pastimes, that is what Americans will do. Elsewhere in the world people have learned to extol marriage as the only innocent sexual relation, while nevertheless failing to live up to it. The important thing for normal un-Americans is to keep up appearances, to acknowledge one's own sinfulness, and to be prepared, when the crunch comes, to give up your lover for your spouse. [French author François] La Rochefoucauld famously described hypocrisy as the tribute that vice pays to virtue. In the sexual mores of today's America [in 2003], however, hypocrisy is regarded as the only genuine sin. Which is why, in America, sexual virtue gets no tributes at all.

"I had to go to Him when I was lonely. If I could be faithful to God during those times, I know I can be faithful to my husband."

Religion Promotes Abstinence Until Marriage

Pamela Toussaint

At age 36, abstinence champion (and former Miss Black California) Lakita Garth kissed her long-time boyfriend for the first time—on their wedding day. In the following viewpoint, Garth discusses how her relationship with God enabled her to stay true to her vow of abstinence until marriage. She also encourages other young women to better appreciate the value of sexual purity, both to themselves and their future husbands. In addition, she comments on the ways in which many Christian congregations are struggling to deal with the topic of abstinence outside of marriage.

As you read, consider the following questions:

1. What perspective on sex outside of marriage did Garth's family have?

Pamela Toussaint, "The 36-Year-Old Virgin, How Abstinence Champion Lakita Garth Kept the Faith During the Long Years Before Her Wedding Night—and Beyond," *Today's Christian*, vol. 44, March–April 2006, pp. 20–23. Reproduced by permission of the author.

2. What scriptural passage did Garth embrace at age 17?

3. What term does the author use to describe people of faith who attempt to convert "nonbelieving" people they are dating to Christianity?

Last summer, 36-year-old Lakita Garth kissed her boyfriend of two years for the very first time—at the altar after they said, "I do."

She and her Mr. Right (literally—her husband's name is Jeffrey Wright) met at a health conference through a mutual friend. "I decided to preach to him, and surprisingly, he didn't go away!" laughs Lakita. When Jeff, a successful Christian publisher in Chicago, was able to spar with her considerable knowledge of biblical doctrine, she became even more intrigued. "I wanted a man who could rise to the challenge, someone I could follow," says Lakita, who was a virgin when she married. "I think women don't have high enough standards. Guys want a challenge, to respect you and to see that you're different. As soon as you start putting out, you lose all of that."

A brainy former beauty queen (she was 1995's Miss Black California), Lakita travels the nation telling "the naked truth" about sexual compromise. She has spoken at countless youth functions, been featured on MTV, and was a regular guest on Bill Maher's *Politically Incorrect*. One of her upcoming books on abstinence until marriage is titled *Give Him the Finger*.

Over two decades, Lakita had many opportunities to compromise her moral standard. However, amid the considerable societal pressure most single adults experience, she was able to stay sexually pure. Her training began early.

It Takes a Family

"In my family, if you had sex outside of marriage, someone got married, or someone got shot!" Lakita recalls with a laugh. Born and raised in a rough part of San Bernardino, Califor-

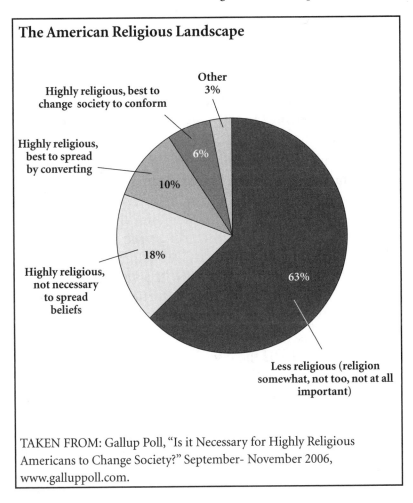

The American Religious Landscape

Other
3%

Highly religious, best to
change society to conform

6%

Highly religious,
best to spread
by converting

10%

18%

Highly religious,
not necessary
to spread
beliefs

63%

Less religious (religion
somewhat, not too, not at all
important)

TAKEN FROM: Gallup Poll, "Is it Necessary for Highly Religious
Americans to Change Society?" September- November 2006,
www.galluppoll.com.

nia, she jokes that her widowed mother slept with two men
every night—Smith and Wesson!

She claims that her "best forms of contraception" were her
four protective brothers. "Growing up, I was taught that rights
and responsibility went hand in hand," she says. "Today,
everyone's demanding rights but no one's talking about responsibility."

The strength of Lakita's extended family played a huge role
in shaping her strong resolve to stay pure, and to make her
life count for Christ. Raised in a then-segregated Alabama, her

uncles and cousins called Dr. Martin Luther King a family friend and frequent guest. "I come from a line of Christians that believe your faith must impact the culture. It has to go farther than your personal relationship with Christ." Self-control, self-discipline, and delayed gratification were staples in Lakita's upbringing, and are the key points she uses when teaching abstinence today [2006].

Despite her strong faith, Lakita did not grow up in the church—she admits that as a child she simply refused to go. "I thought church was where all the hypocrites were," she remembers, though her mother was a faithful churchgoer. Lakita finally made a commitment to Christ at age 17, and says she decided right then that she would live by Isaiah 54:5: "For thy Maker is thine husband". She recalls, "I asked myself, 'If God is really my Husband, then why am I flirting with some guy?' God even knows what I'm thinking!"

Lakita admits there were times when she asked herself other things too, like, Is there something wrong with me 'cause I don't have a boyfriend? Fortunately, her young mind wasn't given much room to explore that question—much of her free time was filled with sports or "cracking the books," and TV was usually off limits in the Garth home. In the long years of single adulthood, Lakita learned how to be comforted by God when she felt alone. "I had to go to Him when I was lonely," she says. "If I could be faithful to God during those times, I know I can be faithful to my husband."

Building Biblical Boundaries

Lakita's ministry is often to teenagers, but she finds Christian adult audiences even more challenging to address on issues of sexual purity. "Christian adults are the most clueless," she notes bluntly. "Many have never heard from the pulpit that sex before marriage is wrong," she says, citing how often singles have come up after her talks and told her so. "The Church needs to start preaching it, and then living it. We need to start equipping folks."

The 2004 Census Bureau's Current Population Survey reports that there are more people in the 30–34 age range who have never been married than there have been since 1970. That means it's likely that there are a greater number of older singles in our churches than we've seen in a long time. But are adult Sunday-school programs, or even church singles ministries, really meeting the needs of older singles? The answers vary, but many church programs seem to be heavy on events, but light on the biblically based teaching relevant to the issues single 30- and 40-somethings face.

Lakita warns single Christian women against "missionary dating," or trying to convert unbelievers while you get emotionally, and too-often physically, entangled. "You can't be the key to his spiritual maturity," she says. Lakita always realized that, because of her strong convictions to be holy, her dating pool would be smaller—which was okay with her. "To be single was to be undistracted in my devotion to God," she says.

When Lakita's relationship with Jeff became serious, they developed boundaries—which she notes many mature singles don't do—and stuck to them. The key to making it work? "The boundaries have to be backed by conviction." She emphasizes that her friendship and business relationship with Jeff was the foundation upon which romantic love blossomed in its proper time.

A Celibate Celebrity

Lakita's testimony of bold sexual purity has garnered much attention, in and out of Christian circles. As a single, she was featured in *Essence* magazine, and last year she shared her just-married bliss with the ladies of ABC's *The View* and readers of *People*. Now, almost a year into married life, she still says, "I'm so glad I waited. Everything is new and exciting. It's like going on a rollercoaster for the very first time!"

Her final word to singles: "Keep your options open." God's perfect mate for you may not look or sound like your "fantasy mate."

> *"Like every human capacity, sexuality is understood as a gift from God and is therefore a legitimate good, provided that it is exercised in faithful acceptance of a divine purpose."*

Religion Encourages Sexuality

Jonathan A. Stein

The following viewpoint asserts that human sexuality is a glorious gift from God that should be treasured, both as a deeply spiritual activity and as a way to experience physical pleasure. According to the author, Judaism teaches that sexual activity is an important path to self-fulfillment, provided that it is explored in a faithful relationship and with an "awareness of God's presence." The author of this viewpoint, Jonathan A. Stein, is a rabbi at Temple Shaaray Tefila in New York City.

As you read, consider the following questions:

1. What is the author's definition of a *Mitzvah*?

2. According to the author, how does Judaism view feelings of lust and sexual fantasies?

Jonathan A. Stein, "Mitzvah: A Liberal Jewish Look at Human Sexuality," *American Sexuality Magazine*, vol. 3, 2004. © National Sexuality Resource Center. Reproduced by permission.

3. Which of the ten proposed elements of liberal Jewish sexual values set forth by the author refer most directly to the importance of sexual pleasure and gratification?

Given the almost 4,000 years of Jewish history since Abraham, "Liberal Judaism," generally understood as one of the attempts to reconcile Jewish tradition and modernity, is a relatively new phenomenon. . . .

Sexuality, on the other hand, is as old as humanity, and is one of the issues that all religions address. Judaism is no exception. From Biblical times until today, Jews have had a lot to say on this subject. Recognizing the importance of trying to articulate an appropriate and relevant approach to sexual behavior in an increasingly sexualized American society, the three liberal Jewish movements . . . have grappled with this subject in recent years.

Traditional Attitude Toward Sexuality

All the movements within Judaism regard appropriate sexual behavior as a *mitzvah*, a sacred human activity potentially imbued with holiness (*kedushah* in Hebrew). Jewish tradition generally views human sexuality as inherently positive and joyous. Like every human capacity, sexuality is understood as a gift from God and is therefore a legitimate good, provided that it is exercised in faithful acceptance of a divine purpose and in reverent awareness of God's presence. Human sexual behavior is understood as both the means to procreation, the fulfillment of the *Torah's* first *mitzvah*, "Be fruitful and multiply. . ." and, in the right context, a way to experience physical delight and pleasure. . . .

In recent decades we have increasingly come to recognize that sexual behavior is always imbued with significance, be that significance physical, moral, emotional, spiritual, or psychological. Human sexual behavior has potential consequences for our self-image and for our relationships with other people.

In our age, irresponsible sexual behavior can too easily lead to disease and death. Judaism teaches that human sexuality reaches its heights in a faithful, covenantal relationship undergirded by a deep emotional commitment, as the ultimate expression of the most intimate of human bonds between two loving people and as a deeply spiritual, not merely physical, activity. If our sexuality is expected to reach its potential for personal fulfillment and moral content, its expression can never be casual.

Because of the many risks that are involved in human sexual behavior, Judaism has historically imposed discipline upon this area of life, setting boundaries and limits that are intended to safeguard both the people involved, and human sexuality itself, from abuse. Judaism has set these limits within the framework of the *mitzvot*. Our tradition's way of thinking about life is distinguished from other religious systems, in part, by the notion of *mitzvah*. In general, the *mitzvot* is a system of ethical and ritual demands based upon the performance of proper behaviors; proper feelings and intentions are not the primary goal. "Our tradition has generally refused to collapse the moral distinction between harboring impious thoughts and feelings and doing irresponsible deeds. One of the marks of moral dignity is the demonstrated capacity to control one's sexual urges." For example, Jewish thought has refused to blur the distinction between (the apparently normal and universal human) feelings of lust and the transformation of lust into specific sexual activity that might be considered immoral. Sexual fantasies, while perhaps not ideal, are not, in and of themselves, considered sinful unless they are acted upon.

Because our tradition is fundamentally oriented toward proper behavior, Judaism has historically deemed it appropriate and even necessary to evaluate human actions. Judaism is not a value free system of thought. Thus sexual conduct, along

Because we treat "sex" as dirty, we associate it with fear and shame, and silence effective sexual education. Public opinion polls consistently demonstrate that Americans want "comprehensive" sexual education—which integrates abstinence education with information on preventing pregnancy and sexually transmitted diseases. At the same time, these polls suggest public confusion about how to achieve sexual literacy. Unfortunately, public opinion is constantly manipulated through misinformation, and sexual conservatives have successfully created moral panics around issues dealing with sexuality.

Our goal is to raise sexual wellness in the United States by promoting sexual literacy. Sexual literacy is an attitude of openness and the desire to learn about sexuality throughout life. Sexually literate people do not mistake packaged sex for genuine sexuality. We need to get back to the basics of better public knowledge and understanding to increase our happiness and enjoyment in life. Sexual literacy is a key to social progress.

> Gilbert Herdt, "A Message from NSRC Director Gilbert Herdt,"
> National Sexuality Resource Center, www.nsrc.sfsu.edu.

with all other behaviors, have been subject to critical evaluation and sometimes harsh judgment.

Liberal Jewish Sexual Values

At the same time, Judaism holds out a number of ideals that undergird the foundation of Judaism's understanding of moral sexual behavior. Among these values are the following:

1. *B'tzelem Elohim* ("in the image of God"). This fundamental Jewish idea is first articulated in Genesis 1:27, "And God created Adam in the divine image . . . male

and female . . ." *B'tzelem Elohim* underscores the inherent dignity of every person and requires us to value one's self and one's sexual partner and to be sensitive to his/her needs. This moral principle demands consent and mutuality in sexual relationships.

2. *Emet* ("truth"). Authentic and ethical human relationships should be grounded in both truth and honesty. Both partners in an intimate relationship should strive to communicate lovingly and candidly. However, honesty that is destructive of the relationship may lack the quality of *rachamim*, mercy. In addition, falsehood that manipulates is sinful.

3. *Brivut* ("health"). Jewish tradition teaches us to rejoice in, and to maximize, our physical, emotional, and spiritual health. Adults of all ages and of all physical and mental capabilities can develop expressions of their sexuality that are both responsible and joyful. The abuse of human sexuality can be destructive to our emotional, spiritual, and physical health.

4. *Mishpat* ("justice"). Judaism insists that it is our duty to reach out and care for others, to treat all of those created in the image of God with respect and dignity, to strive to create equality and justice wherever people are treated unfairly, to help meet the needs of the less fortunate, and to engage in *tikkun olam*, the repair of God's creation. We strive to be sensitive to any abuse of power and victimization of other human beings. All forms of sexual harassment, incest, child molestation, and rape violate the value of *mishpat*. Our pursuit of *mishpat* inspires us to eradicate prejudice, inequality, and discrimination based upon gender or sexual orientation.

5. *Mishpachah* ("family"). The family is a cornerstone of human society and of Jewish life as well. The Torah, through the first *mitzvah* (Genesis 1:28), *p'ru u'rvu*, "be

fruitful and multiply," emphasizes the obligation of bringing children into the world through the institution of the family. In our age, the traditional notion of family is in the process of being redefined. Family also has multiple meanings in an age of increasingly complex biotechnology and choice. The importance of family, whether biologically or relationally based, remains the foundation of meaningful human existence.

6. *Tz'niyut* ("modesty"). The classic *Iggeret HaKodesh*, "The Holy Letter," sets forth the Jewish view that The Holy One did not create anything that is not beautiful and potentially good. The human body in itself is never to be considered an object of shame or embarrassment. Instead, ". . . it is the manner and context in which it (i.e., the body) is utilized, the ends to which it is used, which determine condemnation or praise." Our behavior should never reduce the human body to an object. Dress, language, and behavior should reflect respect for modesty and privacy. As Jews we acknowledge and celebrate the differences between public, private, and holy time, as well as the differences between public, private, and holy places.

7. *Brit* ("covenantal relationship"). For sexual expression in human relationships to reach the fullness of its potential, it should be grounded in fidelity and the intention of permanence. This grounding mirrors the historic Jewish ideal of the relationship between God and the people of Israel, with its mutual responsibilities and its assumption of constancy. A sexual relationship is covenantal when it is stable and enduring and includes mutual esteem, trust, and faithfulness.

8. *Simchah* ("joy"). As a powerful force in human life, sexuality has the potential to bring about physical closeness and pleasure, emotional intimacy and communica-

tion, as well as sexual pleasure and orgasm. Judaism teaches that procreation is not the sole purpose of sexual intimacy; it rejoices in the gratification that sexuality can bring to us. Judaism insists that the joy of human sexual activity should be experienced only in healthy and responsible human relationships.

9. *Ahavah* ("love"). The *mitzvah* from Leviticus 19:18, "You shall love your neighbor as yourself; I am Adonai," serves as an essential maxim of all human relationships. The Hebrew term *Ahavah* is used to describe the ideal relationship between God and humanity, as well as between people. The Jewish marriage ceremony speaks of "*Ahavah v'achavah, shalom v'reiyut*," "love and affection, wholeness and friendship" as ideals that undergird holy relationships. For Jews *Ahavah* is not only a feeling or emotion, but more importantly the concrete behaviors we display toward God and our fellow humans. *Ahavah* implies self esteem, the internal conviction that each of us should appear worthy in our own eyes. *Ahavah* forbids any abuse or violence in sexuality or any aspect of human relationships. *Ahavah* should be expressed through behavior that displays care, support, and empathy.

10. *K'dushah* ("holiness"). This value comes from the root meaning of the Hebrew word *K D Sh*, "distinct from all other, unique, set apart for an elevated purpose." The Torah instructs us: "You shall be holy, for I, Adonai your God, am holy" (Leviticus 19:2). Holiness is not a state of being; rather it is a continuing process of human striving for increasingly higher levels of moral living. In a liberal Jewish context, a relationship may attain a measure of *kedushah* when both partners voluntarily set themselves apart exclusively for each other, thereby finding unique emotional, sexual, and spiritual intimacy. . . .

A liberal Jewish approach to human sexuality reflects the self-consciousness of liberal Judaism generally: the attempt to synthesize a grounding in Jewish tradition with an awareness of the insights of modernity. Because sexuality is such a potent force in human life, this endeavor is particularly difficult. It requires a delicate balance that holds most dear the value of human life. That God has entrusted us with this trial should give us the confidence that we can, indeed, meet the challenge with wisdom and good judgment.

Periodical Bibliography

The following articles have been selected to supplement the diverse views presented in this chapter.

Paul R. Abramson and Steven D. Pinkerton — "Sexual Illiteracy: Why Johnny Can't Make Love," *American Sexuality Magazine*, vol. 3, no. 4, 2007, nsrc.sfsu.edu.

Jane Andrews — "My Daughter's Secret," *Today's Christian*, November–December 2004.

Lilian Calles Barger — "What I Learned from *Sex and the City*: Seeking a Spirituality of the Body," *Sojourners*, August 2004.

Rose Marie Berger — "Managing the Erotic Life," *Sojourners*, May–June 2002.

Scott La Counte — "TV Hook Ups: Television Tells Us Over and Over that Sex Is Fun, but That's Only Part of the Story," *Campus Life's Ignite Your Faith*, March–April 2006.

Daniel C. Maguire — "Sex and the Sacred," *Cross Currents*, Fall 2004.

Rosemary Radford Ruether — "Sexual Illiteracy," *Conscience*, Summer 2003.

Alexa Joy Sherman — "Looking for Love? Uh-Uh" *O, The Oprah Magazine*, October 2004.

Tim Stafford — "Let's Talk Sex: What Christian Books on the Topic Are, and Are Not, Communicating," *Christianity Today*, June 2004.

Arthur Waskow — "Eden and Ethics for a Grown-Up Society: How the Song of Songs Can Give Us a New Sexual Ethic for the 21st Century," *Conscience*, Winter 2005.

OPPOSING
VIEWPOINTS®
SERIES

CHAPTER 2

Should Homosexuality
Be Condemned
on Religious Grounds?

Chapter Preface

In February 2004 more than 4,000 same-sex couples went to city hall in San Francisco, California, and obtained marriage licenses—despite a state ban on gay marriage. Three months after the rush on marriage licenses in San Francisco, which was officially sanctioned and actively encouraged by city mayor Gavin Newsom, hundreds of same-sex couples in Massachusetts began getting married after the U.S. Supreme Court refused to block state legislation giving formal recognition to gay marriage.

These two events triggered an uproar across the nation. In some households and communities, the response was extremely negative: These people saw proof in the events in San Francisco and Massachusetts that the United States had lost its moral bearings and turned its back on God and the Bible. By contrast, the news that some gay American couples were finally securing legal recognition of their unions prompted rejoicing among homosexuals and supportive others who saw these events as just.

The political fallout from these developments came swiftly. During the summer and fall of 2004, eleven states added anti-gay marriage ballot initiatives and referendums to their ballots for the November 2004 election. In every one of these cases, the anti-gay marriage initiative was passed by voters. Moreover, many political observers believe that the intensifying debate over gay marriage motivated conservative voters to go to the polls in such great numbers that they provided the winning margin in President George W. Bush's narrow re-election victory over Democratic nominee John Kerry.

As the following viewpoints indicate, the strong emotions surrounding the issue of gay marriage are unlikely to subside any time soon—and finding common ground on this issue may be difficult. Proponents continue to frame the issue as one of basic fairness and fundamental civil rights, and they increasingly use scripture and the example of Jesus to support their arguments. Opponents, meanwhile, continue to characterize gay marriage as a threat to traditional marriage and an abomination before God, also using scripture in their arguments.

> *"How do you even reason with people who believe that, when something bad happens to [gays], it's God's wrath, but when something bad happens to [straight people], it's God's pop quiz?"*

Religious Opposition to Gay Marriage Is Based on Homophobia

Dan Savage

Many gay and lesbian Americans are convinced that opposition to homosexuality and gay marriage is based primarily on homophobia. In making this argument, they assert that anti-gay rhetoric from religious leaders and organizations is based on selective and dishonest use of scriptural passages. In addition, gay people such as the author of the following viewpoint believe that "faith-based" opposition to gay marriage is hypocritical and damaging to American society. This viewpoint was written by nationally syndicated sex advice columnist Dan Savage in his 2005 book The Commitment. *Savage and his long-time partner have an adopted son.*

As you read, consider the following questions:

1. When Savage claims that Christian conservatives are always "moving the goalposts," what does he mean?

2. Which scriptural passages does Savage cite to illustrate his belief that opponents of homosexuality are dishonest with their use of biblical passages?

3. What point is Savage making when he mentions a 1994 tornado that destroyed a Methodist church in Piedmont, Alabama?

Think about the way many straight people live today. After college, straight men and women move to the big city. Their first orders of business are landing good jobs and finding cool apartments. Then the hunt for sex begins. Most young straights aren't interested in anything serious, so they avoid dating and look for "friends with benefits," or they just "hook up," a.k.a, engage in no-strings-attached sex with anonymous or nearly anonymous partners. Some want to have relationships, but find it hard to make a commitment, so they engage in what's known as "serial monogamy," i.e., they have a series of sexually exclusive, short-term relationships. When they're not having sex, they're going to gyms, drinking, and dancing. And since they don't have kids, these young, hip, urban straight people have lots of disposable income to spend on art, travel, clothes, restaurants, booze and other recreational drugs.

And do you know what all of that hooking up, drinking, and partying used to be called? "The Gay Lifestyle." Substitute "trick" for "hook-up," and "f— buddies" for "friends with benefits," and "unstable relationships" for "serial monogamy," and straight people all over the United States are living the Gay Lifestyle, circa 1978. The only difference is that social conservatives don't condemn straights for being hedonists or attempt to legislate against the straight version of the Gay Lifestyle.

What prompted so many young straights to run off and live like homos? I have a theory: A lot of the early opposition to the gay lifestyle was motivated by envy. Straight people resented gay people for giving themselves permission to do what a lot of straight people wanted to do but couldn't—have fun while you're young, sleep around while you're hot, and live someplace more interesting than the suburbs. When the first post-Stonewall [reference to the famous 1969 clashes between New York City police and patrons of the Stonewall Inn, a gay bar] generation of young straights came to adulthood, they decided they wanted to get in on the action. They could put off having kids and live a little before they settled down. They could be gay, too.

At the same time that young straights were coveting the gay lifestyle, a growing number of gays were coveting the straight lifestyle. While tricks and f— buddies are fun, even hedonism can lose its appeal after a while—particularly after the AIDS crisis drove home the fact that hedonism can have consequences here on earth, not just in some imagined after-life. As individual gays and lesbians matured along with the gay and lesbian civil rights movement, many of us began to realize that we wanted more out of life than tea dances and club nights. . . . Some of us wanted a commitment, a home, maybe some kids. We wanted the Straight Lifestyle.

You would think that after spending three decades arguing that the Gay Lifestyle was a threat to the traditional family because it was so appealingly hedonistic—yes, appealingly, the fear was that straights would be tempted to live like gays, a fear that was not entirely irrational, as it turned out—social conservatives would be delighted when huge numbers of gays and lesbians decided to embrace the Straight Lifestyle and marry. What a victory for traditional family values! So attractive was commitment, so appealing was the prospect of family life, that even gay men and lesbians were embracing them! But unlike all the good-looking straight guys out there who've come to see being lusted after by gay men as a compliment (hello there, Ashton Kutcher), social conservatives refuse to take the compliment. Gay people who want to settle down and live like straights are not an affirmation of the Straight Lifestyle, they insist, just another attack on it.

You would think conservatives would declare victory and take the freakin' compliment. . . . But no. Instead, social conservatives moved the goalposts. From Anita Bryant through early Jerry Falwell, gay people were a threat because we didn't live like straight people. Now we've got Rick Santorum and late Jerry Falwell running around arguing that gay people are a threat because some of us do live like straight people. It's not on the hedonism charge that the religious right has attempted to move the goalposts. Anti-gay leaders used to argue that homosexuality was so disgusting a perversion that not even animals engaged in it. When researchers admitted that many other animals—from white-tailed deer to pygmy chimpanzees to hooded warblers—engage in homosexual sex acts and, in some instances, form lasting homosexual bonds, anti-gay leaders declared that gay sex was a disgusting perversion *because* animals engaged in it. I suspect that Kathleen Parker, the conservative commentator who accuses gay parents of being "selfish," would condemn me for being a selfish, self-indulgent gay man if I were childless and spending $1,000 a month on, say, male prostitutes in leather hot pants and not on [son] D.J.'s school tuition.

The religious right moves the goalposts so often that they sometimes forget where they were left last.

The religious right still levels the hedonism charge when it suits them. Robert H. Knight, director of the Culture and Family Institute, a conservative Christian group, attempted to pin the blame for skyrocketing housing costs on gays and lesbians in an interview with a Christian news service. "The homosexual lifestyle is about pleasing oneself," Knight said, "not planning for the future, not setting aside money for the kids, not creating a situation where the generations come together. It's about having fun. It's about indulging in whatever desire you want at any given time." With no kids or generations to worry about, we have more money to spend on housing, and drive up home prices.

Or maybe there are multiple sets of anti-gay goalposts on the field. Homosexuals who do set aside money for the kids and bring the generations together are a threat to the American family; homosexuals who don't do those thing are a threat to the American family's home.

And all those straight people living the Gay Lifestyle in cities like New York, Chicago, Boston, San Francisco, Los Angeles, Atlanta, Miami, Seattle, Portland—basically any city with a population over 250,000? Social conservatives don't have much to say about their hedonism. They want to prevent gay people from acting like straight people (by banning same-sex marriage, gay adoptions, civil unions, and domestic partnerships), but there's no concurrent effort to ban straight people from acting like gay people. This hardly seems fair. If we can't get married, at the very least, all the straight people who've moved into gay neighborhoods should have to go back to the 'burbs, where they should be forced to marry young and make babies. If we can't have marriage, can we at least have our neighborhoods, gyms, bars, and lifestyle back?. . .

If gays living like straights and straights living like gays proves anything, it's that there really is no such thing as "The Gay Lifestyle"—or "The Straight Lifestyle," for that matter. My life proves there's nothing inherently "straight" about making a commitment or starting a family; my brother Billy's life proves there's nothing inherently gay about being urban and childless and having an "understanding." (Although it is fun to accuse Billy of being a bigger fag than I am.) The Straight Lifestyle was only "straight" because gay people weren't allowed to form lasting relationships, or to have families, things we weren't allowed to do because for centuries straight people insisted we were incapable of it. And how did straight people know we couldn't form lasting relationships? Because we didn't form them. And why didn't we? Because discrimination, hatred, and bigotry warped our lives. Until very recently it was illegal for us to have relationships at all. You could be jailed for being openly gay, your family could have you committed, you could be lobotomized. And our relationships—all conducted under the threat of imprisonment, some conducted post-lobotomy—because *these* relationships weren't perfect in every possible way, that imperfection used to justify the very persecution that warped our lives in the first place. . . .

We also weren't sure we were prepared to sacrifice the one thing gay relationships have always had over straight relationships: their quiet dignity.

Before gay marriage became an option, no one expected a same-sex couple to put on a floor show for our families and friends about how much we really, truly loved each other. Straight couples that want their relationships to be taken seriously have always had to jump through the marital hoop, but not gay couples. We couldn't cut to the front of the take-my-relationship-seriously line by getting married two days or two months or two years after we met. Unlike heterosexuals, we had to do the hard work of building a life together in order to be taken seriously, something we did without any legal entanglements or incentives. Without the option of making a spectacle out of our commitment—no vows, no cakes, no rings, no toasts, no limos, no helicopters—we were forced to simply live our commitments. We might not be able to inherit each other's property or make medical decisions in an emergency or collect each other's pensions, but when our relationships were taken seriously it was by virtue of their *duration*, by virtue of the lives we were living, not by virtue of promises we made before the Solid Gold Dancers jumped out of the wedding cake at the reception.

My relationship with Terry has always been our own creation, the product of a love some people believe isn't even
supposed to exist. With state and church against us, there's a
kind of dignity in loving each other anyway. Sometimes when
we're introduced as a couple, straight couples will ask how
long we've been together. Often they're shocked and delighted
to learn that we've been together such a long time. At first I
assumed many were shocked because they believed that gay
men weren't good at forming stable relationships. But when
I've pried—and I tend to pry—I've found myself listening to
straight people explain that it means something different to
them when a gay couple hangs in there long enough to get
into the double digits. We could walk away from each other at
any time, but we don't. That can mean only one thing: We really, truly love each other. Married straight couples don't benefit from the same assumption. They might stay together for
love or they might stay together because they take their vows
seriously, because they do see themselves as "bound together
in holy matrimony." They've tied the knot and the bitch in the

house is stuck with the bastard on the couch. Divorce is an option, of course, but the awareness of how awful an experience divorce is works to keep some couples together.

Yes, yes: The quiet dignity of a long-term gay relationship isn't worth the stigma of being treated as second-class citizens. The inability of stable, long-term gay couples to tie the knot is discriminatory and unfair. A straight couple could meet and marry in one drunken evening in Las Vegas (how about a constitutional amendment to put a stop to that?), and their relationship has more legal standing than, say, the fifty-one-year relationship of Phyllis Lyon and Del Martin, the first same-sex couple to marry in San Francisco. Then there's Julie and Hillary Goodridge, one of the same-sex couples who successfully sued the state of Massachusetts for the right to marry. They'd been together seventeen years on their wedding day. If a groom in Las Vegas were to be hit by a car leaving the chapel with his bride, his new wife—not his parents, not his siblings—would have the legal right to direct his medical care and, if necessary, pull the plug. But after fifty-one years, Phyllis and Del may not be able to make those end-of-life decisions for each other. Distant cousins who might be hostile to the surviving partner could blow into town and make all the medical decisions. While the arrival of gay marriage will correct this injustice, something else will be lost, something intangible, something that used to be uniquely our own. . . .

It's not just exhaustion that has many American gays and lesbians eyeing the exits, but a real fear of where the Republican right's never-ending campaign against gays and lesbians will ultimately lead. Republicans tell their religious supporters that the existence of gays and lesbians is a threat to the American family, western civilization, and, as influential conservative Christian leader James Dobson claimed, "the survival of the earth." We're godless commies, marauding Visigoths, and global warming all rolled up into one great big mirrored disco ball.

You typically hear one of two things when you press a Dobson supporter about the threat that homosexuality supposedly presents to the planet. "The practice of homosexuality is potentially lethal to the human race," Rev. Rolfe F. Westendorf wrote in *The Northwest Lutheran*, a religious paper. "It is activity which precludes the possibility of procreation. Hence, if everyone were gay, the human race would be finished in fifty years."

The assumption at the base of the "if everyone were gay . . ." argument is a compliment, if a back-handed one. People like Dobson and Westendorf apparently believe that homosexuality is so tempting that pretty soon no one is going to want to be heterosexual. A sane person might think that the long, sordid history of heterosexuality, and the current human population of six billion, is all the evidence we need that human beings will never tire of heterosexual sex, but not Dobson or Westendorf.

And what of all those straight people out there who live near, work beside, and hang out with gays and lesbians for years without ever succumbing to our charms? I've shared an office with a straight guy for eight years, and he's still sleeping with women; according to *New York* magazine, straight women are still finding husbands in Manhattan; and the last time I was in San Francisco, I actually saw a man and a woman making out in a cab. If heterosexuality can thrive in seemingly inhospitable places like my office, Manhattan, and San Francisco, it's a hardier weed than hysterics like Dobson and Westendorf give it credit for being.

The other argument for the threat homosexuality presents to the planet is harder to refute. God hates gays—it's right there in the Bible, along with "God hates shrimp" (Leviticus 11:9–12), "God hates poly-cotton blends" (Leviticus 19:19), "God approves of slavery" (Exodus 21:20–21; Ephesians 6:5–6), "God wants you to pay your taxes without griping about it" (Matthew 22:17–21), and "God approves of killing women and children" (Deuteronomy 2:33–34). God destroyed Sodom and Gomorrah because of the homos, Christian conservatives insist, and if we're not careful we're going to reach some sort of mincing critical mass and God will lose his shit and destroy the planet. God is already mighty annoyed with current levels of gay and lesbian activity on our planet and, according to prominent Christian conservatives, He's trying to let us know. Sitting in a hotel room in Portland, Oregon, I listened to a "Christian leader" on a cable news shoutfest describe the December 26, 2004, earthquake and tsunami that killed a quarter of a million people in Asia as evidence of God's displeasure. With Asians? No, with same-sex marriage. "We can't allow things that offend God to flourish without expecting to incur the wrath of God," she said. She cited gay and lesbian marriages in Canada, San Francisco, and Massachusetts. "Gay marriage offends God deeply," hence the killer wave.

God may be all-knowing and all-powerful, but He is, it seems, a lousy shot, the [nearsighted 1950s cartoon figure] Mr. Magoo of higher powers. Same-sex couples get married in Boston, Toronto, and San Francisco, and a vengeful, nearsighted God triggers an earthquake that slams a killer wave into Indonesia, Thailand, India, and Sri Lanka, killing a quarter of a million people who weren't even invited to the wedding.

But perhaps I'm being unfair to God: Sometimes He does manage to score a direct hit. The 1993 Northridge Earthquake, measuring 6.7 on the Richter scale, scored a direct hit to the San Fernando Valley in Los Angeles, California. Christian conservative leader Pat Robertson was quick to blame the multi-billion-dollar porn industry, which is based in the San Fernando Valley, for an earthquake that took fifty-seven lives and caused billions of dollars in damage. God doesn't like pornography, you see, and while not one of the people who died that day was a porn star, a porn director, or a porn producer, God's message was clear: Stop making dirty movies in the San Fernando Valley or I'll drop some more houses on innocent bystanders.

The funny thing about God and natural disasters, though, is that He sometimes strikes the faithful, too. So we can only wonder about what, exactly, God's message was on March 27, 1994. Less than three months after God slapped the San Fernando Valley with an earthquake, God slammed a tornado into a church in Piedmont, Alabama. The Goshen Methodist Church was completely destroyed during Palm Sunday services. Twenty people were killed and ninety were injured. Among the dead was the four-year-old daughter of the pastor. The same Christian conservatives who pointed to the earthquake that hit Los Angeles as a condemnation of the porn industry, and a decade later claimed that the Asian tsunami was God's vote against same-sex marriage, get awfully quiet when the subject of the Piedmont Palm Sunday Tornado is raised. The best they can do is this: God was testing the faith of His flock.

How do you even reason with people who believe that, when something bad happens to you, it's God's wrath, but when something bad happens to me, it's God's pop quiz?

"There are absolutely no grounds for considering homosexual unions to be in any way similar or even remotely analogous to God's plan for marriage and family."

Religious Opposition to Gay Marriage Is Based on Scripture

The Vatican (Cardinal Joseph Ratzinger)

Since gay marriage and civil unions first emerged as subjects of debate, the Roman Catholic Church has consistently voiced its opposition to the idea. This viewpoint from the Vatican, released in mid-2003 with the formal approval of then-Pope John Paul II, cites a range of scriptural and practical reasons for opposing homosexual unions. This viewpoint was written by Cardinal Joseph Ratzinger, head of the Vatican's Congregation for the Doctrine of Faith. After Pope John Paul II died on April 2, 2005, Ratzinger was elected to succeed him. The papacy of Ratzinger, who took the name Pope Benedict XVI, began on April 19, 2005.

The Vatican (Cardinal Joseph Ratzinger), "Considerations Regarding Proposals to Give Legal Recognition to Unions Between Homosexual Persons," *Congregation for the Doctrine of the Faith*, June 3, 2003. Reproduced by permission.

As you read, consider the following questions:

1. What scriptural passages does the Vatican cite in describing homosexual acts as "a serious depravity"?

2. What impact would homosexual unions have on the "social order," according to the document?

3. What justifications does the Vatican statement use to oppose the legal arguments for recognition of homosexual unions?

In recent years, various questions relating to homosexuality have been addressed with some frequency by Pope John Paul II and by the relevant Dicasteries of the Holy See [Vatican bodies that assist the Pope and his pastoral mission]. Homosexuality is a troubling moral and social phenomenon, even in those countries where it does not present significant legal issues. It gives rise to greater concern in those countries that have granted or intend to grant—legal recognition to homosexual unions, which may include the possibility of adopting children. The present Considerations do not contain new doctrinal elements; they seek rather to reiterate the essential points on this question and provide arguments drawn from reason which could be used by Bishops in preparing more specific interventions, appropriate to the different situations throughout the world, aimed at protecting and promoting the dignity of marriage, the foundation of the family, and the stability of society, of which this institution is a constitutive element. The present Considerations are also intended to give direction to Catholic politicians by indicating the approaches to proposed legislation in this area which would be consistent with Christian conscience. Since this question relates to the natural moral law, the arguments that follow are addressed not only to those who believe in Christ, but to all persons committed to promoting and defending the common good of society.

The Nature of Marriage

The Church's teaching on marriage and on the complementarity of the sexes reiterates a truth that is evident to right reason and recognized as such by all the major cultures of the world. Marriage is not just any relationship between human beings. It was established by the Creator with its own nature, essential properties and purpose. No ideology can erase from the human spirit the certainty that marriage exists solely between a man and a woman, who by mutual personal gift, proper and exclusive to themselves, tend toward the communion of their persons. In this way, they mutually perfect each other, in order to cooperate with God in the procreation and upbringing of new human lives.

The natural truth about marriage was confirmed by the Revelation contained in the biblical accounts of creation, an expression also of the original human wisdom, in which the voice of nature itself is heard. There are three fundamental elements of the Creator's plan for marriage, as narrated in the Book of Genesis.

In the first place, man, the image of God, was created "male and female" (*Gen* 1:27). Men and women are equal as persons and complementary as male and female. Sexuality is something that pertains to the physical-biological realm and has also been raised to a new level—the personal level—where nature and spirit are united.

Marriage is instituted by the Creator as a form of life in which a communion of persons is realized involving the use of the sexual faculty. "That is why a man leaves his father and mother and clings to his wife and they become one flesh" (*Gen* 2:24).

Third, God has willed to give the union of man and woman a special participation in his work of creation. Thus, he blessed the man and the woman with the words "Be fruitful and multiply" (*Gen* 1:28). Therefore, in the Creator's plan, sexual complementarity and fruitfulness belong to the very nature of marriage.

Furthermore, the marital union of man and woman has been elevated by Christ to the dignity of a sacrament. The Church teaches that Christian marriage is an efficacious [effective] sign of the covenant between Christ and the Church (cf. *Eph* 5:32). This Christian meaning of marriage, far from diminishing the profoundly human value of the marital union between man and woman, confirms and strengthens it (cf. *Mt* 19:3–12; *Mk* 10:6–9).

There are absolutely no grounds for considering homosexual unions to be in any way similar or even remotely analogous to God's plan for marriage and family. Marriage is holy, while homosexual acts go against the natural moral law. Homosexual acts "close the sexual act to the gift of life. They do not proceed from a genuine affective and sexual complementarity. Under no circumstances can they be approved."

Sacred Scripture condemns homosexual acts "as a serious depravity . . . (cf. *Rom* 1:24–27; *1 Cor* 6:10; *1 Tim* 1:10). This judgment of Scripture does not of course permit us to conclude that all those who suffer from this anomaly are personally responsible for it, but it does attest to the fact that homosexual acts are intrinsically disordered." This same moral judgment is found in many Christian writers of the first centuries and is unanimously accepted by Catholic Tradition.

Nonetheless, according to the teaching of the Church, men and women with homosexual tendencies "must be accepted with respect, compassion and sensitivity. Every sign of unjust discrimination in their regard should be avoided." They are called, like other Christians, to live the virtue of chastity. The homosexual inclination is however "objectively disordered" and homosexual practices are "sins gravely contrary to chastity."

God's True Design for Marriage

The advocates of same-sex marriage say they believe in God—most seek to invoke His name in their marriages. I say it's time for everyone to stop—stop and ask ourselves: "Was God wrong?" God's definition of marriage is clearly defined in the account of His creation of this basic human relationship in Genesis 2: 22–24:

> And the rib, which the Lord God had taken from man, made he a woman, and brought her unto the man. And Adam said, "This is now bone of my bones, and flesh of my flesh: she shall be called Woman, because she was taken out of Man. Therefore shall a man leave his father and his mother, and shall cleave unto his wife: and they shall be one flesh.

Was God wrong in creating woman and man for each other? Was he wrong when he established marriage as the institution in which children are to be born?

God's design for marriage is the only one that matters. The evidence . . . also proves that God's design for marriage is the only one that works for mankind.

God loves us—all of us. He created mankind in His own image, and designed a beautiful framework in which we can thrive and multiply and experience true fulfillment in every sense of the word. The laws of nature—created and defined by the Creator—are the indisputable evidence that fundamental to mankind's societal existence is the cornerstone of marriage between one man and one woman.

To say otherwise is to declare God wrong.

Rebecca Hagelin, "Was God Wrong?"
WorldNet Daily, *May 18, 2004, www.worldnetdaily.com.*

The Vatican Position on Homosexual Unions

Faced with the fact of homosexual unions, civil authorities adopt different positions. At times they simply tolerate the phenomenon; at other times they advocate legal recognition of such unions, under the pretext of avoiding, with regard to certain rights, discrimination against persons who live with someone of the same sex. In other cases, they favour giving homosexual unions legal equivalence to marriage properly so-called, along with the legal possibility of adopting children.

Where the government's policy is *de facto* [in fact] toler-ance and there is no explicit legal recognition of homosexual unions, it is necessary to distinguish carefully the various as-pects of the problem. Moral conscience requires that, in every occasion, Christians give witness to the whole moral truth, which is contradicted both by approval of homosexual acts and unjust discrimination against homosexual persons. There-fore, discreet and prudent actions can be effective; these might involve: unmasking the way in which such tolerance might be exploited or used in the service of ideology; stating clearly the immoral nature of these unions; reminding the government of the need to contain the phenomenon within certain limits so as to safeguard public morality and, above all, to avoid expos-ing young people to erroneous ideas about sexuality and mar-riage that would deprive them of their necessary defences and contribute to the spread of the phenomenon. Those who would move from tolerance to the legitimization of specific rights for cohabiting homosexual persons need to be reminded that the approval or legalization of evil is something far differ-ent from the toleration of evil.

In those situations where homosexual unions have been legally recognized or have been given the legal status and rights belonging to marriage, clear and emphatic opposition is a duty. One must refrain from any kind of formal cooperation in the enactment or application of such gravely unjust laws and, as far as possible, from material cooperation on the level of their application. In this area, everyone can exercise the right to conscientious objection.

Other Arguments Against Homosexual Unions

To understand why it is necessary to oppose legal recognition of homosexual unions, ethical considerations of different orders need to be taken into consideration.

From the order of right reason

The scope of the civil law is certainly more limited than that of the moral law, but civil law cannot contradict right reason without losing its binding force on conscience. Every humanly created law is legitimate insofar as it is consistent with the natural moral law, recognized by right reason, and insofar as it respects the inalienable rights of every person. Laws in favour of homosexual unions are contrary to right reason because they confer legal guarantees, analogous [roughly the same] to those granted to marriage, to unions between persons of the same sex. Given the values at stake in this question, the State could not grant legal standing to such unions without failing in its duty to promote and defend marriage as an institution essential to the common good.

It might be asked how a law can be contrary to the common good if it does not impose any particular kind of behaviour, but simply gives legal recognition to a *de facto* reality which does not seem to cause injustice to anyone. In this area, one needs first to reflect on the difference between homosexual behaviour as a private phenomenon and the same behaviour as a relationship in society, foreseen and approved by the law, to the point where it becomes one of the institutions in the legal structure. This second phenomenon is not only more serious, but also assumes a more wide-reaching and profound influence, and would result in changes to the entire organization of society, contrary to the common good. Civil laws are structuring principles of man's life in society, for good or for ill. They "play a very important and sometimes decisive role in influencing patterns of thought and behaviour." Lifestyles and the underlying presuppositions these express not only externally shape the life of society, but also tend to modify the younger generation's perception and evaluation of forms of behaviour. Legal recognition of homosexual unions would obscure certain basic moral values and cause a devaluation of the institution of marriage.

From the biological and anthropological order

Homosexual unions are totally lacking in the biological and anthropological elements of marriage and family which would be the basis, on the level of reason, for granting them legal recognition. Such unions are not able to contribute in a proper way to the procreation and survival of the human race. The possibility of using recently discovered methods of artificial reproduction, beyond involving a grave lack of respect for human dignity, does nothing to alter this inadequacy.

Homosexual unions are also totally lacking in the conjugal dimension, which represents the human and ordered form of sexuality. Sexual relations are human when and insofar as they express and promote the mutual assistance of the sexes in marriage and are open to the transmission of new life.

As experience has shown, the absence of sexual complementarity in these unions creates obstacles in the normal development of children who would be placed in the care of such persons. They would be deprived of the experience of either fatherhood or motherhood. Allowing children to be adopted by persons living in such unions would actually mean doing violence to these children, in the sense that their condition of dependency would be used to place them in an environment that is not conducive to their full human development. This is gravely immoral and in open contradiction to the principle, recognized also in the United Nations Convention on the Rights of the Child, that the best interests of the child, as the weaker and more vulnerable party, are to be the paramount consideration in every case.

From the social order

Society owes its continued survival to the family, founded on marriage. The inevitable consequence of legal recognition of homosexual unions would be the redefinition of marriage, which would become, in its legal status, an institution devoid of essential reference to factors linked to heterosexuality, for example, procreation and raising children. If, from the legal standpoint, marriage between a man and a woman were to be considered just one possible form of marriage, the concept of marriage would undergo a radical transformation, with grave detriment to the common good. By putting homosexual unions on a legal plane analogous to that of marriage and the family, the State acts arbitrarily and in contradiction with its duties.

The principles of respect and non-discrimination cannot be invoked to support legal recognition of homosexual unions. Differentiating between persons or refusing social recognition or benefits is unacceptable only when it is contrary to justice. The denial of the social and legal status of marriage to forms of cohabitation that are not and cannot be marital is not opposed to justice; on the contrary, justice requires it.

Nor can the principle of the proper autonomy of the individual be reasonably invoked. It is one thing to maintain that individual citizens may freely engage in those activities that interest them and that this falls within the common civil right to freedom; it is something quite different to hold that activities which do not represent a significant or positive contribution to the development of the human person in society can receive specific and categorical legal recognition by the State. Not even in a remote analogous sense do homosexual unions fulfil the purpose for which marriage and family deserve specific categorical recognition. On the contrary, there are good reasons for holding that such unions are harmful to the proper development of human society, especially if their impact on society were to increase.

From the legal order

Because married couples ensure the succession of generations and are therefore eminently within the public interest, civil law grants them institutional recognition. Homosexual unions, on the other hand, do not need specific attention from the legal standpoint since they do not exercise this function for the common good.

Nor is the argument valid according to which legal recognition of homosexual unions is necessary to avoid situations in which cohabiting homosexual persons, simply because they live together, might be deprived of real recognition of their rights as persons and citizens. In reality, they can always make use of the provisions of law—like all citizens from the standpoint of their private autonomy—to protect their rights in matters of common interest. It would be gravely unjust to sacrifice the common good and just laws on the family in order to protect personal goods that can and must be guaranteed in ways that do not harm the body of society. . . .

The Church teaches that respect for homosexual persons cannot lead in any way to approval of homosexual behaviour or to legal recognition of homosexual unions. The common good requires that laws recognize, promote and protect marriage as the basis of the family, the primary unit of society. Legal recognition of homosexual unions or placing them on the same level as marriage would mean not only the approval of deviant behaviour, with the consequence of making it a model in present-day society, but would also obscure basic values which belong to the common inheritance of humanity. The Church cannot fail to defend these values, for the good of men and women and for the good of society itself.

> *"The legal issue of marriage should be separated from the church—as it used to be. . . . That should be left to the civil authorities. . . . Then religious couples, heterosexual or same-sex, could approach the church of their choice to seek a religious blessing."*

Civil Unions Are an Acceptable Alternative to Gay Marriage

Jim Wallis

Jim Wallis, who is a theologian, bestselling author, and editor in chief of Sojourners *magazine, claims that both opponents and advocates of gay marriage have staked out unreasonable positions. In the following viewpoint, he asserts that both sides refuse to acknowledge the realities that do not support their positions. Wallis urges both sides to drop their unyielding positions and suggests that civil unions might be an acceptable compromise. He also insists that whatever the outcome of the gay marriage debate, Christians have a moral obligation to welcome gays and lesbians into the "community of faith."*

Jim Wallis, *God's Politics: Why the Right Gets It Wrong and the Left Doesn't Get It.* New York: HarperSanFrancisco, 2005, pp. 329–335.

As you read, consider the following questions:

1. How does the author see the current state of marriage and family life in America?

2. What is Wallis's chief criticism of "the Left" regarding its views of the relationship between family and social problems?

3. What is the author's chief criticism of "the Right" regarding its views of the relationship between family and social problems?

Family and "family values." Seldom has the importance of an issue been so great, and seldom has the political manipulation of it been even greater. The bonds of family that tie together our most important and intimate relationships and provide the critical framework for raising the next generation are too important to be reduced to mere symbols in our most partisan and bitter political wars. Yet that is precisely what has happened. Liberals and conservatives, Democrats and Republicans are all responsible for politicizing the questions of family life and thus contributing to the disastrous weakening of this most basic and important institution.

Each of us, across the political spectrum, must now recognize the crisis of family life in America. The statistics are overwhelming and simply demand our attention. Nearly half of all marriages end in divorce, 1.5 million women a year are assaulted by their current or former husbands or boyfriends, one in three children are born outside marriage (even in poor communities), and so on. Family ties and relationships are growing weaker at an alarming pace, with disastrous consequences—especially for children. And the consequences are also clear for poverty; delinquency and crime; sexual promiscuity; education and employment; physical, emotional, and mental health; spiritual well-being; and social pathologies that transmit themselves intergenerationally. Family breakdown figures into a wide variety of other social problems as a primary causal factor.

But as soon as the issues of family breakdown are raised as a public issue, a very ideological debate quickly ensues about the ideal forms of family life that various cultural, religious, or political constituencies wish to advance. What is soon lost are the "facts" of family life and how those facts can be either weakened or strengthened.

Defining "Family"

There have been many forms of family in history, the most common being the extended family where blood relationships across generations create strong webs of social networks and living arrangements, which provide security and stability for all its members, and multiple role models guide the young. The extended family is arguably the most historically common form of family life and is undoubtedly the form of family operative in ancient biblical cultures, both Jewish and Christian. Of course, forms of extended family life, some stronger and some weaker, continue today as most families have networks of broader relations.

But the more modern phenomenon of "the nuclear family" is what most today refer to as family and is the particular result of a modern industrial and consumer society. Because they have fewer resources to draw upon, nuclear families are more subject to many pressures and tensions that can be more easily absorbed in the extended family model. Today [2005], many forces undermine nuclear families and thus imperil family life as most people in our cultures experience it. And today, there are new forms of family life emerging: single-parent families, families that skip a generation with grandparents having the primary child-rearing responsibilities, some same-sex couples rearing children, and cohabiting couples of unmarried heterosexual adults who choose not to marry but may also be raising children (often from previous marriages). And more people are divorced, widowed, and otherwise living alone than ever before. All of these forms of family have their impact on children.

In the fall of 2003, the Massachusetts Supreme Court ruled that gay and lesbian couples in that state are legally entitled to marry, thereby entitling them to the same "legal, financial, and social benefits" as heterosexual couples. That decision set off a great controversy that played a prominent role in the 2004 election debate. The city of San Francisco and other jurisdictions began issuing marriage licenses to same-sex couples, and President Bush announced his support for a constitutional amendment to stop gay marriages—which were then being performed by the thousands in both San Francisco and Massachusetts. The issue was joined. The topic now seems destined to continue as one of the most controversial issues in America for some time to come.

Over the past decade, this "family values" question has become very difficult and has been polarized by both the religious Right and the cultural Left. To move forward, we must simply refuse the false choices offered by both sides.

As we have already noted, the Left has often misdiagnosed the roots of our present social crisis, mostly leaving out the critical dimension of family breakdown as a fundamental component of problems like poverty and violence. These issues are not important just to the religious Right and are not simply bourgeois [materialistic middle-class] concerns. We do need to rebuild strong and healthy two-parent families. And we desperately need more strong male and female role models in both "nuclear" and extended families.

Today, family breakups, broken promises, marital infidelity, bad parenting, child abuse, male domination, violence against women, lack of living family wages, and the choice of material over family values are all combining to make the family norm in America more and more unhealthy. A critical

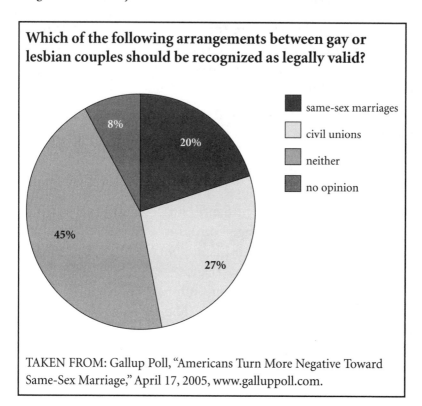

Which of the following arrangements between gay or lesbian couples should be recognized as legally valid?

■ same-sex marriages

□ civil unions

■ neither

■ no opinion

8%

20%

45%

27%

TAKEN FROM: Gallup Poll, "Americans Turn More Negative Toward Same-Sex Marriage," April 17, 2005, www.galluppoll.com.

mass of healthy families is absolutely essential to the well-being of any society. That should be clear to us by now, especially in neighborhoods where intact families have all but disappeared.

But the Right has seized upon this agenda and turned it into a mean-spirited crusade. To say gay and lesbian people are responsible for the breakdown of the heterosexual family is simply wrong. That breakdown is causing a great social crisis that affects us all, but it is hardly the fault of gays and lesbians. It has very little to do with them and honestly more to do with heterosexual dysfunction and, yes, "sin." Gay civil and human rights must also be honored, respected, and defended for a society to be good and healthy. It is a question of both justice and compassion. To be both pro-family and pro-gay civil rights could open up some common ground that might take us forward.

Do we really want to deny a gay person's right to be at their loved one's deathbed in a hospital with "family restrictions"? Do we also want to deny that person a voice in the medical treatment of his or her partner? And do we really want all the worldly possessions of a deceased gay person to revert to the family that rejected them thirty years ago, instead of going to their partner of the last twenty years? There are basic issues of fairness here that can be resolved with or without a paradigm shift in our basic definition of marriage.

We can make sure that long-term gay and lesbian partnerships are afforded legitimate legal protections in a pluralistic society no matter what our views on the nature of marriage are. But the question of gay marriage is important; it is a major issue in the religious community, and it is unlikely to be resolved for many years. Many in the churches and the society believe that the long-standing and deeply rooted concept of marriage as being between a man and a woman should not be changed, but same-sex couples should be granted the rights of "civil unions." That's still my own view. For others, only gay marriage fulfills the requirements of equal protection under the law. There are at least three different views being debated in the churches. Most Christians still believe that the sacrament and theology of the church on marriage should not be altered, while others are exploring new rites of church "blessings" for gay and lesbian couples committed to lifelong relationships, and still others want full sacramental inclusion.

The states themselves will ultimately resolve the legal and civil issues through referendums and legislative proceedings. While the issues of gay civil rights are fundamental matters of justice in a democratic society, the legal and ecclesial questions of how to handle the specific marriage issue should not be used to divide the churches, as too many on both the religious Right and religious Left seem eager to do.

In 2004, *Sojourners* published a dialogue between two seminary presidents, Richard Mouw of Fuller Theological

Seminary and Barbara Wheeler of Auburn Theological Seminary. One is more conservative on the issues of homosexuality, the other more liberal. Both are members of the Presbyterian Church USA, which like many other denominations, threatens to divide over the issue. But Mouw and Wheeler believe that would be a mistake.

Richard Mouw says:

> I hope with all my heart that we can avoid the divorce court. I want us to stay together. I do not have a clear sense of what it would take to avoid what many of our fellow Presbyterians apparently are convinced is an inevitable separation. I do sense, however, a strong need to keep talking. The church, some insist, is not some mere voluntary arrangement that we can abandon just because we do not happen to like some of the other people in the group. God calls us to the church, and that means that God requires that we hang in there with each other, even if that goes against our natural inclinations. I agree with that formulation.

> I want with all my heart for this to happen to us in the Presbyterian Church—that we take up our arguments about the issues that divide only after we have knelt and laid our individual and collective burdens of sin at the foot of the cross. Needless to say, if it did happen, I would be surprised. But then, the God whom we worship and serve is nothing if not a God of surprises.

Barbara Wheeler says:

> How's this for a model of the church that we are called to become: "They confessed that they were strangers and foreigners on the earth." What if instead of denying our estrangement, or bemoaning it, we embraced it as a gift from God?

> A church that contains members we think strange, even barbaric, is a healthier setting for us, for our formation as Christians. We like to think that a church of our kind, one

that excludes those who believe incorrectly and behave badly by our lights, would be a better school for goodness than the mixed church we've got. It is not necessarily so. Familiarity and affinity breed bad habits as well as virtues.

The last and most critical reason for all of us Presbyterian strangers to struggle through our disagreements is to show the world that there are alternatives to killing each other over differences. As long as we continue to club the other Presbyterians into submission with constitutional amendments, judicial cases, and economic boycotts, we have no word for a world full of murderous divisions, most of them cloaked in religion.

I believe that the protection of gay civil rights should be a bottom line in the debate, and I try to say that especially in very conservative evangelical circles. On the issues of gay marriage, our *Sojourners* magazine has not taken a "position" but rather an "approach" of civil dialogue between Christians who are committed to justice and compassion but who have different understandings of how best to resolve the question of gay marriage. It is our view that while gay civil rights is a fundamental justice issue, the controversies over gay marriage and the ordination of gay bishops, and so on, should not be seen as "faith breakers." The church is going to have to learn to stay together and talk about these things until we find some resolutions together. Many feel that legal protections can and should be extended to same-sex couples, without necessarily changing our whole definition of marriage. But one could also argue that gay civil marriage is necessary under "equal protection." One could also argue for church blessings of gay unions. I think all those are strong points, even if the churches are unlikely to change their whole theology and sacrament of marriage itself. But this is the good and necessary dialogue. And in the meantime, the church must stand up for gay and lesbian people under attack and must welcome them into the community of faith.

Evangelical leader Tony Campolo offers one proposal. While taking the conservative view that the Bible does not affirm homosexual practice, Campolo denounces homophobia and supports gay civil rights. But he believes that the legal issue of marriage should be separated from the church—as it used to be. Clergy should no longer pronounce marriage blessings "by the authority vested in me by the State of Pennsylvania." That should be left to the civil authorities, and both heterosexual and gay couples should apply to the state for the civil right—be it civil marriage or civil union. Then religious couples, heterosexual or same-sex, could approach the church of their choice to seek a religious blessing. Most churches will only provide marriage ceremonies for the union of a man and a woman. But there are a growing number of local congregations that are open to offering blessings to same-sex couples. It is a solution that might satisfy most, as it preserves the Christian conscience of diverse positions. But for it to work, those congregations that open up to gay couples should not be cut off from their denominations, and neither should more traditional churches be pressured to accept gay marriage by liberal voices in their own denominations.

Conservative Christians should be careful not to draw their primary line in defense of family at the expense of gay couples who want to make a lifelong commitment, instead of standing prophetically against the cultural, moral, and economic forces that are ripping families apart. And liberal Christians should not just argue for gay marriage on the grounds of human rights, but rather should probe more deeply into the theological, biblical, and sacramental issues that are also at stake.

When conservatives seem to suggest that the future of western civilization is at stake in the battle over the legal status of same-sex couples, they seriously overstate the issue. Likewise, when liberals say that resolving the legal issues surrounding gay unions is morally equivalent to the issues of racism, apartheid, and the Holocaust, they make the same mistake. Solutions to the definitional legal issues for gay couples will eventually be found, but this is not the ultimate moral confrontation of our time, as partisans on both sides have tried to make it. It will take many years before we are able to better understand and resolve the many complicated factors surrounding the issue of homosexuality. When we do, we should be able to look back and feel good about the way we conducted our dialogue and our relationships in the process.

> "To offer civil unions as the compromise
> position is, in effect, to concede that the
> debate really is about civil rights rather
> than an aggressive campaign to trans-
> form the culture by replacing the tradi-
> tional family as the cornerstone of so-
> cial order. . . ."

Civil Unions Are Not an Acceptable Alternative to Gay Marriage

Peter Wood

*In this viewpoint, a conservative scholar argues that civil unions
will wreak just as much damage on traditional family structures
and American society as gay marriage. Viewpoint author Peter
Wood also urges opponents of civil unions to do a better job of
explaining how legally recognized unions of same-sex couples
constitute a serious threat to future generations of Americans.
Wood was a professor of anthropology at Boston University in
2004 when this viewpoint was published. Wood is currently [as
of 2007] provost of The King's College in New York City, where
he is also professor of anthropology and the humanities.*

Peter Wood, "What's So Civil About Civil Unions?" *www.nationalreview.com*, February
17, 2004. Reproduced by permission.

As you read, consider the following questions:

1. What is the basic marriage rule followed by the Miwuyt tribe of aborigines in Australia?

2. According to Wood, the movement to legalize civil unions and gay marriage is not really about gay marriage. What does he think it actually is about?

3. What quote from Michel De Montaigne does the author use to illustrate his belief that compromise is not always wise?

A banner headline in the *Boston Globe* last week [February 2004] was, "Lawmakers Eye Civil Union Provision." The Massachusetts legislature is soon to decide whether to advance a proposed Defense of Marriage Amendment in a compromise form that would allow gay couples civil unions instead of marriage. At issue is whether the amendment proposed by state representative Philip Travis has to be watered down to gain the votes it needs to pass at the constitutional convention that opened last week and resumes in March.

The political temperature is rising in Massachusetts in a drama that may well be replayed in other states as well as in this year's presidential election (including California, if San Francisco's recent exercise in civil disobedience, allowing gay couples to "marry" is any indication). The anti-gay-marriage group Let the People Vote is running advertisements against legislators who support gay marriage. House speaker Thomas Finneran is weighing a decision to defy the Massachusetts Supreme Judicial Court by promoting a bill to prohibit the issuance of same-sex-marriage licenses. And even the *Boston Globe* is finally taking note of critics, such as Princeton University Professor Jeffrey Satinover and Amherst College Professor Hadley Arkes, who have been pressing the point that the establishment of gay marriage will lead the way to further developments such as polygamy.

Where is the sensible moral and political ground on these matters? There is clearly a potential rift between conservatives who oppose both gay marriage *and* civil unions, and those who wish to concentrate on prohibiting gay marriage, more or less conceding on civil unions. The debate over the Federal Marriage Amendment is drawing some conservatives to the position that, in order to build a coalition in support of the amendment, the issue of civil unions should be left to the states. But here in Massachusetts we do not have the option of putting off that day of reckoning. Should the state constitutional convention strike for the compromise? I am edging the other way. I don't think enacting civil-unions laws will prevent the kinds of damage that gay marriage itself would inflict on our society. The unhappy social consequences would be the same either way.

Civil Unions in Scandinavia

Stanley Kurtz's analysis of how gay civil unions in Scandinavian countries have contributed to the decline of heterosexual marriage and the rise of out-of-wedlock births ought to be the foundation of further discussion of these matters. Civil unions in Scandinavia came in the wake of social developments that had already weakened marriage but they added decisive new elements: a final sundering of the connection between "marriage" and having children, and a demoralization of the old institutional supporters of marriage, including many of the churches.

Kurtz has given us a careful prying apart of the many layers of the Scandinavian reality. It is not that, one day, the Scandinavian governments enacted civil-unions laws and the next day heterosexual marriage collapsed. But if we follow Kurtz through his account piece by piece, civil unions emerge as a distinctive force with their own path of social consequences. The Scandinavian countries, in effect, have run an experiment in which they have taken to its logical extreme the idea of the British sociologist Anthony Giddens that modern marriage is simply about elective companionship. If that is all marriage is, why get married? The Swedes, the Danes, and the Norwegians can't seem to think of any compelling reason. The Scandinavian gay civil-unions laws distinguish civil unions from marriage in respect to a handful of rights, such as access to artificial insemination. The Vermont version of civil unions eliminates even those distinctions and offers in effect the definitive declaration by the state that nothing—absolutely *nothing*—distinguishes random sexual coupling from official marriage.

These Scandinavian laws are primarily symbolic since not many Scandinavian gays actually get civil-unionized, but that's not to say that such laws are irrelevant. Culture, as we anthropologists are wont to say, is comprised of symbols. Change the symbols and you change the culture.

The Miwuyt Marriage Rule

While I admire Kurtz's willingness to spend many months sifting through demographic statistics and getting obscure sociological articles translated from Danish and Norwegian, I have been thinking about peoples more remote from traditional Western institutions. On the north coast of Australia in the area known as Arnhem Land live several thousand Australian aborigines. Historically they lacked a collective name for themselves and anthropologists supplied the lack with various terms: the Murngin, the Wulamba, the Miwuyt, and most recently the Yolngu. They made news in the 1970s by successfully suing the Australian government over the appropriation of their land for bauxite mines. Their rich tradition of bark cloth painting has now involved them in the international art market. But they are probably still best known in anthropological circles for their remarkable marriage system.

The basic Miwuyt marriage rule is that a man should marry his mother's mother's brother's daughter's daughter

(MMBDD). When I teach this to my anthropology students, the inevitable first question is, "What if he doesn't have one?" But, of course, he always does. The Miwuyt know perfectly well how to operate their marriage system so that it does what they want it to. Or rather, the older Miwuyt men know how to operate the system—for it turns out that the polygamous Miwuyt elders manage to collect numerous brides. The key is a certain flexibility in classifying relatives as MMBDDs even if they are not literally so. Some men have upwards of ten wives, many of whom are much younger than their husbands. Anthropologists have characterized the system as a kind of gerontocracy.

As far as I know, gay marriage and civil unions aren't anywhere in the Miwuyt scheme of things. The Miwuyt, however, serve as an excellent example of the difference between abstract rules governing marriage ("Marry your MMBDD.") and social realities. And recognition of that difference seems sorely lacking in much of the debate over gay marriage and civil unions.

Gay Marriage as a Civil Right?

When the Massachusetts Supreme Judicial Court decided on November 18 [2003] that the state is obligated to extend the benefits of marriage to gay and lesbian couples, it framed the matter wholly as a set of abstract rights. To a large extent the ensuing debate has pitted defenders of traditional marriage against champions of a new "civil right." The champions of gay marriage, in other words, have immediate access to the powerful ideal and rhetoric of human equality, while the defenders of traditional marriage are equipped mainly with an assortment of religious arguments, appeals to tradition, worries about possible side effects like the rise of polygamy, and a general but vague apprehension that is all too easily caricatured by gay rights proponents as mere prejudice.

It is not prejudice at all. That apprehension is an inarticulate insight that gay marriage or civil unions would, in some deep sense, transform marriage for everyone. But exactly how? The Miwuyt, in far-away Arnhem Land, offer a clue. Marriage for the Miwuyt involves complicated reciprocities of clans and generations, organized into a "section" system that has baffled anthropologists for 70 years, along with the prescription of marrying one's MMBDD. But draw back from the precise details and it is plain enough that the system works to benefit the older males and reinforce their dominance over women and younger males.

Unmasking the True Agenda

Likewise, the "civil-rights" issue mainly obscures what gay marriage (and civil unions) would do. The gay-marriage movement isn't really about gay marriage at all. Stable gay and lesbian couples already exist and with only a little inconvenience can arrange for themselves virtually all the "rights" and conveniences that come with marriage. Rather the gay-marriage debate is fundamentally about making homosexual behavior a fully accepted and legitimate part of American life. Gay marriage, like civil unions in Scandinavia, is a symbolic device aimed at transforming this aspect of our culture.

Having to argue this out in the form of a debate on "gay marriage" may be a good thing, in that at least it frames the matter of re-valuing homosexuality as a specific issue. But it is, of course, the battleground and the timing chosen by the Left. Homosexuality has already won cultural approval in the mass media from television shows to the nuptial announcements in the *New York Times*, and in many other contexts, including many churches. The gay-marriage debate is, in that sense, intended as the final battle, after which full normalization of homosexuality will be a matter of cleaning up some details.

And I don't believe conservatives have yet devised a winning defense. Certainly not if we begin with a preemptive surrender on "civil unions." To offer civil unions as the compromise position is, in effect, to concede that the debate really is about civil rights rather than an aggressive campaign to transform the culture by replacing the traditional family as the cornerstone of social order with an amorphous category of sexual liaisons. Eliminate the normative family in the U.S., and who benefits? The Scandinavian situation offers a pretty good clue. Junk the family and its functions will necessarily be transferred to the state: to state day-care centers, welfare bureaucracies, and government agencies. But as long as we continue to debate gay marriage on the grounds preferred by the Left—as a civil-rights issue—the larger assault on the traditional family anchored on the sexual, emotional, and practical complementarity of one man and one woman will remain invisible.

The Perils of Compromise

Conservatives at this juncture seem faced with a choice of strategies: whether to emphasize the recklessness of the proponents of gay marriage in their willingness to jeopardize traditional marriage for what appears to be, at best, a modest social gain; or whether to emphasize the much larger cultural question of the place of homosexuality in our society. The public and political debate, though limited, has been carried on by people like Maggie Gallagher and Stanley Kurtz, almost entirely within the frame of the former position, i.e., "We need to defend marriage." I agree, we do, and Gallagher and Kurtz have made excellent arguments. But I somehow doubt that their arguments are connecting with as a large a public as they hope. Can the other argument ("We should not allow marriage to be used to give full legitimacy to homosexuality.") do better? Can we make both arguments?

Recently, about 4,000 people rallied on the Boston Common in opposition to gay marriage. I talked afterwards to one of the protesters who seemed rather discouraged. He noted that, as he has gone around and talked to people in the state about the issue, he has found many who are diffident [timid]. They have essentially bought the line, "Why should I care? If two gay people get married, how does that hurt me?" In truth, it probably wouldn't. The destructive consequences would fall mainly on the young and the vulnerable who would grow up in a society without the bulwark of traditional marriage protecting them against the excesses of their own immature appetites and the rapacious desire of older males ever eager to expand the zone of sexual permissiveness.

But how do we get that message across? An acquaintance, David Boyajian, who is active in the Massachusetts fight against gay marriage, observed that civil unions are winning support in the polls and from pundits [experts] as the "third way" between gay marriage and outright prohibition. Frame an issue as a three-way choice, he observes, and the middle term almost automatically gets adopted as the moderate, sensible choice. He jests: "Do you favor executing [or] hanging ALL, SOME, or NONE of the people who object to gay marriage?"

All: 23%

Some: 42%

None: 25%

But the Boyajian Principle seems sound. It is not so hard to imagine the poll that will ask, "Do you think polygamy should be prohibited, optional, or mandatory?" But perhaps this game can be turned around. I think we should press for a poll on a question such as, "Should civil unions be available to same-sex couples, organized labor, or Australian marsupials?"

Jesting with calamity has some merit, but it probably won't change the tenor of the debate. As to whether we should cut our losses by accepting civil unions as a step short of gay marriage, I take counsel from Michel De Montaigne. In his essay "On Vain and Cunning Devices," Montaigne warns against the illusion that the middling way is always safest. Rather the middle ground is the natural home of "erroneous opinions" and men who "bring disturbances to the world." I think we are best off facing the harder question squarely. To be generous in spirit and worthy as a culture, do we really need to abandon our commitment to traditional marriage? That's where gay marriage—and civil unions too—will inexorably take us.

Periodical Bibliography

The following articles have been selected to supplement the diverse views presented in this chapter.

Nate Blakeslee — "Family Values," *Texas Monthly*, March 2007.

Bernadette Brooten — "How Our Minds Have Changed: A Historical View of Same-Sex Love," *Conscience*, Spring 2006.

Howard Dean — "Vermont's Lessons on Gay Marriage," *Boston Globe*, May 17, 2004.

Alphonse de Valk — "Same-Sex Marriage: The Battle Against God and Country," *Catholic Insight*, July–August 2006.

Maggie Gallagher — "Banned in Boston: The Coming Conflict Between Same-Sex Marriage and Religious Liberty," *Weekly Standard*, May 15, 2006.

Mary E. Hunt — "A Marriage Proposal: With Gay Marriage Now on the Agenda, It May Be Time to Consider the Institution of Marriage Itself," *Conscience*, Summer 2006.

Christopher Lisotta — "Radical Islam in Your Backyard," *Advocate*, May 23, 2006.

Amy McDougall and Jake Nyberg — "Gay Rights Activists Seek—and Find—Dialogue on (Some) Christian Campuses," *Sojourners*, September–October 2006.

Irene Monroe — "We Who Are Left Behind," *Advocate*, May 9, 2006.

Online NewsHour — "The Battle over Same Sex Marriage," January 2, 2007, www.pbs.org/newshour/bb/law/gay_marriage.

Jonathan Rauch — "A Separate Peace," *Atlantic Monthly*, April 2007.

CHAPTER 3

Is a Belief in God Incompatible with Reproductive Rights?

Chapter Preface

On April 18, 2007, the U.S. Supreme Court upheld by a 5–4 vote the first federal law that bans an abortion procedure for all women and all doctors in all states. This court decision upheld the legality and constitutionality of the federal Partial-Birth Abortion Ban Act, which had been mired in Court battles since its passage in 2003. This act banned a rarely used abortion procedure—known as "partial-birth" by abortion foes and "dilation and evacuation" by doctors—that is most often used in pregnancies where the mother's health is judged to be at risk. The U.S. Supreme Court decision overturned the opinions of three lower federal courts that had held that the 2003 act was unconstitutional because it does not provide a "health exception" for pregnant women facing a medical emergency.

Reaction to the U.S. Supreme Court decision was swift and emotional. President George W. Bush spoke for many pro-life organizations and individuals opposed to abortion when he said that the Court's official sanction of the 2003 act "represents a commitment to building a culture of life in America." Pro-choice organizations denounced the decision and echoed the words of dissent from Justice Ruth Bader Ginsburg, who declared that the majority's opinion in the case was "alarming" and could not "be understood as anything other than an effort to chip away a right [to abortion] declared again and again by this Court, and with increasing comprehension of its centrality to women's lives."

Many observers believe that the war of words about the meaning and impact of the federal ban on "partial-birth" abortions will intensify in coming years. Since the 1973 U.S. Supreme Court Roe v. Wade decision legalizing abortion in the United States, the abortion issue has polarized political parties, communities, families, and religious organizations. But until relatively recently, *Roe v. Wade* has seemed firmly entrenched in U.S. law. The Supreme Court verdict on the Partial-Birth Abortion Ban Act has shaken that assumption, and both sides of the debate recognize that the next few years are likely to determine the reproductive choices and freedoms available to American women for generations to come. In the following viewpoints, religious men and women from both sides of the abortion debate offer their perspectives of the stakes involved.

> "No woman chooses to be in a situation
> in which she must consider an abor-
> tion, but if that is the decision a
> woman has to make, I believe firmly
> that God is with her in that moment."

Christians Should Support Abortion Rights

Reverend Dr. Roselyn Smith-Withers

In the following viewpoint, Baptist minister Roselyn Smith-Withers takes issue with the assumption that most girls and women who decide to have abortions are wracked with guilt afterward. She also explains her deep conviction that God stands with girls and women who have abortions and that pro-choice beliefs are not incompatible with Christian faith. Smith-Withers is a Baptist pastor at the Pavilion of God in Washington, DC, and a member of the Clergy Advisory Committee of the Religious Coalition for Reproductive Choice.

As you read, consider the following questions:

1. According to the author, what is the primary emotion that women feel after an abortion?

Reverend Dr. Roselyn Smith-Withers, "Testimony: Hearing on The Impact of Abortion on Women," *Subcommittee on Science, Technology and Space of the U.S. Senate Committee on Commerce, Science, and Transportation*, March 3, 2004. Reproduced by permission of the author.

2. What is the author's view of Christian denominations and groups that oppose abortion?

3. Why does the author see the consequences of "unintended childbearing" as being so severe?

Thank you for the opportunity to present testimony today on the important issue of the impact of abortion on women. I am Reverend Dr. Roselyn Smith-Withers, Co-Convener of the Clergy Advisory Committee of the Religious Coalition for Reproductive Choice (RCRC) and founder and pastor of The Pavilion of God in Washington D.C. The Religious Coalition for Reproductive Choice (RCRC), founded in 1973, is a national non-profit education and advocacy organization whose members are national bodies from 15 denominations and faith traditions with official positions in support of reproductive choice, including the Episcopal Church, Presbyterian Church (USA), United Church of Christ, United Methodist Church, Unitarian Universalist Association, and Reform and Conservative Judaism.

As an ordained clergyperson and clergy counselor trained in the Religious Coalition model of counseling called All Options Clergy Counseling, I have counseled many women over the last 15 years. Some women have spiritual and religious concerns as they consider their options. My goal in counseling is to help women discern what is right and best for them and their family and to help them come to an understanding that they believe is consistent with their faith and conscience. Women with an unintended or unplanned pregnancy have many different feelings and concerns as they consider their options and after they have decided on a course of action and taken that action. I tell women that there are no easy answers as to what to do, that they must weigh everything involved in this decision—whether they are prepared for parenthood, have the family and financial support they need, are physically and emotionally able to handle the challenges, and many other

A Pro-Choice Message for Jewish Congregations

The Religious Right would like the American public to believe that for one to be religious, one must necessarily also be anti-choice. In reality, many religious leaders worked toward legalizing abortion long before *Roe v. Wade*. During the 1960s, horrified by the injuries and death suffered by women around the country due to illegal, unsafe abortions, they responded as people of faith and conscience must. Reverend Howard Moody and Arlene Carmen organized the first Clergy Consultation Service in New York City, a network of clergy who agreed to help women gain access to safe abortion providers. Similar services soon developed throughout the country.

It was during this time that the progressive movements within Judaism began to advocate for a liberalization of abortion laws. Because Jewish law and tradition allows for abortion, it becomes a matter of religious freedom for American Jews that the secular government not be involved in these personal moral decisions. This one sentence in the United States Constitution, "Congress shall make no law respecting an establishment of religion, or prohibiting the free exercise thereof," has been the foundation of the success of the Jewish community in this country. Without this guarantee, we would be mere guests in this country, as we have been in so many other countries throughout our history, living at the sufferance of the rulers and of our neighbors.

Religious Coalition for Reproductive Choice, "A Sermon for Jewish Congregations," www.rcrc.org/perspectives/sermons/jewish.cfm.

considerations that they know best. I assure them that, while a problem or unintended pregnancy can be devastating, it can also mark the beginning of a more mature life because it requires that they take charge of their own future. In my experience, women become stronger when they are able to make these most personal, morally complex decisions for themselves, without fear and without coercion. No woman chooses to be in a situation in which she must consider an abortion, but if that is the decision a woman has to make, I believe firmly that God is with her in that moment.

The Need for Abortion Rights

Women, both unmarried and married, become pregnant unintentionally for various reasons, including rape and date rape, failed birth control, and lack of information about contraception and sexuality. Many of these women experience a point of low esteem, some even wanting to die. Later, they can come to understand that they can heal and that their faith can be part of that healing.

Research has shown that, while some women may experience sensations of regret, sadness or guilt after an abortion, the overwhelming responses are relief and a feeling of having coped successfully with a difficult situation. Yet the idea persists that women must be guilt-ridden by an abortion and that the decision will haunt them for the rest of their lives. There is an unfounded and unexamined presumption that a woman's conscience guides her not to have an abortion. In my experience as a counselor, I have more often seen women who are guided by their conscience and their sense of responsibility to have an abortion. Because abortion is so stigmatized, they do not express their true feelings and desires. The stigmatization of unplanned pregnancy and abortion can have a coercive effect, causing some women to continue a pregnancy that they prefer to terminate, with lifelong consequences to the woman and her family. Clergy who are trained in the All Options counseling model and who counsel women before and after abortions know that most women believe they have made a responsible decision.

Research studies support what women know in their hearts: that women's emotional responses to legal abortion are largely positive. In 1989, the American Psychological Association (APA) convened a panel of psychologists with extensive experience in this field to review the data. They reported that the studies with the most scientifically rigorous research designs consistently found no trace of "post-abortion syndrome" and furthermore, that no such syndrome was scientifically or medically recognized. The panel concluded that "research with diverse samples, different measures of response, and different times of assessment have come to similar conclusions. The time of greatest distress is likely to be before the abortion. Severe negative reactions after abortions are rare and can best be understood in the framework of coping with normal life stress." Adler pointed out that despite the millions of women who have undergone the procedure since 1973, there has been no accompanying rise in mental illness. "If severe reactions were common, there would be an epidemic of women seeking treatment," she said.

In May 1990, a panel at the American Psychiatric Association conference argued that government restrictions on abortion are far more likely to cause women lasting harm than the procedure itself.

Abortion Is a Moral Choice

To insist, as do groups that oppose abortion in all cases, that women who have an abortion are devastated as a result simplifies the complex nature of each woman's feelings. Even worse, such pronouncements induce and nurture guilt, undermine women's self-respect, and convince women they must be forgiven for a sin, even though abortion might be the most responsible, moral decision.

Religious women who have had abortions have very different feelings from those described by groups that oppose abortion. The book *Abortion, My Choice, God's Grace*, by Anne

Eggebroten, tells the stories of women who have had abortions. Elise Randall, an evangelical Christian and graduate of Wheaton College, who had an unwanted pregnancy, said, "I was filled with resentment and afraid that I might take out my frustrations on the child in ways that would do lasting damage." She and her husband concluded that abortion "was the most responsible alternative for us at this time. The immediate result was an overwhelming sense of relief. Now we were free to deal with the existing problems in our lives instead of being crushed by new ones ... Only God knows what might have been, but I like to think that our decision was ... based on responsibility and discipleship."

Christine Wilson, an active member of a Presbyterian church in suburban Baltimore and attorney, wife and mother of two grown children, became pregnant when she was 16 after having sex for the first time with her boyfriend. At first naïve and then later embarrassed and afraid, she did not tell her parents until she was five months pregnant. Because abortion was illegal at that time, her father took her to England for the abortion. For many years she suffered in silence from guilt and emotional turmoil. Now, she says, "If I had (legal) access in 1969, I know it would not have taken 25 years to attain the peace of mind I have today."

The Campaign to Stigmatize Abortion

The attempt to stigmatize abortion and the women who have had abortions is so far-ranging that it can be considered a campaign. Medical groups calling themselves pro-life, whose purpose is to promote misinformation about abortion, are active and growing; these groups use the professional credibility of doctors to promote a political agenda that includes opposition to emergency contraception and insurance coverage of contraceptives. The campaign is also strong in some Christian denominations, in which groups or caucuses have formed to reverse traditional church policies that support reproductive choice as an act of conscience. The website of the National Organization of Episcopalians for Life (NOEL), for example, which calls itself a "para-church organization within the Anglican tradition," states that the group seeks to change "the growing 'culture of death' in America and the Episcopal Church," in contrast to the resolution adopted by the church's 1994 General Convention that "Human life, therefore, should be initiated only advisedly and in full accord with this understanding of the power to conceive and give birth that is bestowed by God." The National Silent No More Awareness Campaign of NOEL and Priests for Life work to make abortion "unthinkable" while the Episcopal Church, in another statement adopted by its official body, urges there be "special care to see that individual conscience is respected and that the responsibility of individuals to reach informed decisions in this matter is acknowledged and honored."

It is important and heartening to all who care about women's health and lives to know that the consensus in the medical and scientific communities is that most women who have abortions experience little or no psychological harm. The claim that abortion is harmful is not borne out by the scientific literature or by personal experiences of those who counsel women in non-judgmental, supportive modalities such as All Options Clergy Counseling. In fact, scientific data shows that the risk for severe psychological problems after abortion is low and comparable to that of giving birth.

The Negative Impact of Unintended Childbearing

Yet while there is extensive political and media discussion of the supposed harm caused by abortion, the negative effects of unintended childbearing are basically ignored. Yet they have enormous consequences for women, children and families, and society at large. A recent study documents the negative effects of unintended childbearing on both the mother and her family. Women who have had unwanted births sustain lower quality relationship with all of their children, affecting the children's development, self-esteem, personality, educational and occupational attainment, and mental health and future marital relationships. Mothers with unwanted births are substantially more depressed and less happy than mothers with wanted births. The negative effects of unintended and unwanted childbearing persist across the course of life, with mothers with unwanted births having lower quality relationships with their children from late adolescence throughout early adulthood.

In conclusion, as a clergy counselor I believe that women such as Elise Randall and Christine Wilson, whose stories were recounted in Eggebroten's book, deserve respect for making a complex decision. As their experiences indicate, it is not the abortion that can cause harm but the negative attitudes of others, including those who oppose abortion for personal, political, ideological or other reasons. Women who have an unintended pregnancy and decide to have an abortion need our compassion and support. To help women and families, we should work together to reduce unintended pregnancies through increased access to family planning and emergency contraception, comprehensive sexuality education, quality health care, and compassionate counseling.

> *"In . . . the fight against abortion, we*
> *see displayed with perfect clarity the*
> *principle of a single upright truth (that*
> *directly killing an unborn child is an*
> *evil and a crime) being contested by a*
> *rotation of errors. . . ."*

Christians Should Not Support Abortion Rights

Todd M. Aglialoro

This viewpoint claims that the pro-choice movement has pur-
sued several strategies to obscure the moral bankruptcy of abor-
tion. The author identifies five specific pro-choice arguments that
he sees as irrelevant, cynical, or intellectually dishonest. He as-
serts, however, that none of these approaches provides convincing
arguments that abortion can be a moral choice. The author of
this viewpoint is Todd M. Aglialoro, editor of Sophia Institute
Press, a publisher of books about Catholicism and the Catholic
faith.

As you read, consider the following questions:

1. What impact did the 1980 film *The Silent Scream* have
   on the abortion debate, according to the author?

2. What is the author's response to Mario Cuomo's arguments?

3. According to the author, which side in the abortion debate most prefers to inject religion into the debate?

In that passage from *Orthodoxy* so familiar that it is almost now cliché, G.K. Chesterton wrote that there are a thousand angles at which a man may fall but only one at which he stands. By this he argued for the unique, enduring character of orthodox Church doctrine, of the one, true, upstanding strand of Right Teaching. Though the same tired heresies may reappear to contest it—mutated, renamed, warmed-over—the old, wild truth remains standing, "reeling but erect."

This well-worn lesson takes on a new freshness, I think, when applied to the culture war. The wild truths that inform Christian ethics—our insistence on a moral universe, on a real human nature with its own teleology, on the transcendent significance of human acts and human relationships—also reel but remain erect in the face of perennial challenges. We are not gods. Moral truth is something we discover, not invent. From the Garden of Eden to the Supreme Court of the United States, we have fought the same battle under different banners.

In what is probably the modern culture battle par excellence, the fight against abortion, we see displayed with perfect clarity the principle of a single upright truth (that directly killing an unborn child is an evil and a crime) being contested by a rotation of errors; taking turns or working in tandem, passing in and out of fashion, each seizing upon the vocabulary, events, and moods of the cultural moment until the next comes along to supplant it.

In some cases cultural developments render one of them obsolete. In the years shortly after *Roe v. Wade* [the 1973 Supreme Court ruling that legalized abortion], abortion debates inevitably featured three words the pro-abortion side considered a trump card: "blob of tissue." This factually empty but sound-bite-perfect catchphrase made a great impact with its implication that the fetus was roughly equivalent to a ball of snot. Which put abortion about on par with picking your nose: bad form, a messy affair that ought to be kept private, but nothing to get overly excited about.

Of course, advances in the study of human embryology, most notably the window to the womb afforded by the sonogram, all but pulled the teeth from the "blob of tissue" canard [misleading story]. The 1980 film *The Silent Scream*, an ultrasound depiction of an abortion at eleven weeks, provided a chilling, graphic look at abortion's inner workings. And today, expectant mothers keep pictures of their "blobs of tissue" on the refrigerator. They make copies and stuff them into Christmas cards.

So that particular line was no longer viable. But it wouldn't be the last. More would follow, and we who are engaged in the culture have surely heard most of them. However, even for those who have heard them all, I think it can be valuable to gather them up and define them; to identify their originators, exemplars, and champions; to understand their appeal; and to consider how to counter them. Let us now look, then, at five (a nice number, though by no means exhaustive) of history's most insidious pro-abortion arguments. . . .

Avoiding the Word "Abortion"

Early last year [2003], in a calculated PR [public relations] move, the National Abortion Rights Action League (NARAL) changed its name to NARAL Pro-Choice America. Amazingly, the new name is even more cumbersome than the old. "NARAL" juts out at the front like "Nokia" before "Sugar Bowl." But this name change was not about streamlining signage and business cards. It was an attempt to deflect notice from the singular object of NARAL's 30-plus years of existence—unlimited access to abortion-on-demand—and toward broader, more high-minded, and less gruesome concepts of gender equality and personal self-determination. The change was timed to coincide with a multimillion-dollar ad campaign depicting the new-and-improved NARAL not so much as an advocate of "abortion rights" as a defender of women's suffrage, satellite TV, and 31 Flavors.

Semantic games have always been part of the battle, of course. No one—*no one*, mind you—is "pro-abortion." Folks are "pro-choice," "pro-reproductive rights," or, slightly more courageously, "pro-abortion rights." In each case, even the last, the emphasis is steered away from the repugnant reality of abortion itself—a sure loser in focus groups time and time again. Whenever we debate abortion or write a letter to the editor, we engage in a struggle for the linguistic high ground. . . .

It can be wearying sometimes, but the counter-strategy is continually to return the debate to where it belongs: the humanity of the unborn child and his right to life. It may also be effective to ask just why abortion is so repugnant to so many.

The "Personally Opposed" Tactic

It is these days thoroughly engrained in abortion discourse, its premises taken for granted and its logic never questioned. It is all too common for a politician, clergyman, or fellow parishioner to claim that he is "personally opposed" to abortion but wouldn't dream of "imposing" that opinion on a public with diverse religious and ethical beliefs—and then sit back, secure in the feeling that his is an ironclad position.

Yet this line about being "personally opposed, but. . ." has only the appearance of reasonableness, acquired through sheer repetition. It also fits perfectly in a society valuing tolerance above all other virtues, conflict-avoidance over tackling unpleasant truths. . . .

In a 1984 speech at the University of Notre Dame titled "Religious Belief and Public Morality," [former governor of New York Mario] Cuomo laid out the basic premises of the "personally opposed, but. . ." line, by way of reconciling his soi-disant [so-called] devout Catholicism with his political support for abortion-on-demand. Skillfully equivocating Catholic teaching on abortion with Catholic teaching on contraception and divorce, as well as a presumed Catholic perspective toward nuclear weapons, he asks, would it be right for a Catholic to make (or sign) laws forbidding divorce? Withholding state funds for contraception? Instituting a unilateral nuclear freeze?

"Should I argue," he asks, "to make my religious value your morality? My rule of conduct your limitation?" Clearly not, is his conclusion. Not, absent a democratic consensus, in a society of varied and sometimes flatly contradictory moral values, a society in which even the collective voice of Christianity is not monolithic on issues but fractured and sectarian. Not, he notes, when "there is no Church teaching that mandates the best political course for making our belief everyone's rule, for spreading this part of our Catholicism."

The forceful case made by Cuomo in his speech (he quotes for support, in places, Michael Novak and even Pope John Paul II; the whole thing makes for fascinating reading) touches only on the context of politics, and mostly from the politician's perspective. But its spirit has crept out of the corridors of power into general society. It is the spirit that makes the saying "If you don't like abortion, don't have one" sound to some ears like a devastating rejoinder. The spirit that gives rise to slogans like "You can't legislate morality," when in fact the morality that protects human rights and thus the common good is the first and best thing worth legislating.

It is also the spirit that animates our next argument.

The True Lesson of Feminism

We insist on informed consent for appendectomies or tooth extractions, but not abortions. As a result, American daughters now coming of age will see only the go-girl aspect of sexual freedom without the whoa-mama revelation of maternal awe.

The latter isn't learned from a textbook, but is experienced during that moment of personal reckoning when one realizes that a fetus is unequivocally a baby. My own transformative thinking—from an unflinching pro-choicer to a disclaiming pro-lifer—came with childbirth and motherhood.

After experiencing the humbling power of creation, it was impossible for me to view abortion as anything but the taking of a life. That is the truer lesson feminism should impart to its little sisters.

Kathleen Parker, "Abortion Chic,"
October 6, 2006, www.townhall.com.

The "Safe, Legal, and Rare" Argument

Among politicians only Bill Clinton could devise a line like this, during his 1996 campaign, brilliantly triangulating liberal abortion-on-demand orthodoxy with Middle America's broad-based distaste for the practice. Ultimately nonsensical yet somehow familiar and reassuring, like a couplet from Dr. Seuss [pen name of Theodor Geisel, author of children's books], this buzz phrase became an instant and enduring success, for two reasons.

First, it validated the internal conflict that the majority of Americans were (and still are) experiencing over the abortion question. They were conscious of a natural sense of revulsion toward abortion itself, yet unwilling for whatever reason to sign on whole-hog with the pro-lifers. Clinton let them know that he felt their pain and that his administration's policy would include a subtle nod toward the general feeling that abortion is a Bad Thing (which ought to be "rare") but would not place restrictions on its availability ("legal") that might send women to back alleys ("safe"). Thus he accomplished an unprecedented political feat: co-opting the vaguely antiabortion sentiments of the masses and mollifying the blood lust of the radical pro-abort left with one simple statement.

"Safe, legal, and rare" also subtly but definitely realigned the terms of the abortion debate. No longer would the question center on whether the aborted fetus was a blob or a baby; no longer would it be necessary to make tortured distinctions between public and private morality. In the first place, safety and legality are conservative concepts, not radical ones. Now the pro-choicer could consider himself a guardian of the status quo—an American tradition, even. In the second place, with the word "rare," the focus shifted away from abortion itself (which we now presumed to be beyond debate) and toward abortion's presumptive root causes. The abortion issue was now *really* a health-care or poverty or education issue—right in the liberal Democrats' wheelhouse.

To be truly pro-life, they could argue, meant to "get over this love affair with the fetus" (as former Surgeon General Jocelyn Elders put it, with typical elegance) and instead pay attention to alleviating the conditions that led women to get abortions in the first place. Implied here, of course, is a kind of false dichotomy: The qualities of justice and mercy are not strained, nor must the interests of the mother and unborn child be necessarily set at odds. But the argument worked by playing into multiple stereotypes: pro-lifers as single-issue fanatics, misogynists, icy-hearted grinches. And it allowed politicians to spin abortion questions into Great Society sermonettes. . . .

Mourning as an Option

In [the 1995 essay] "Our Bodies, Our Souls," [feminist writer Naomi] Wolf called for "a radical shift in the pro-choice movement's rhetoric and consciousness about abortion." Self-deluded by their long practice of dehumanizing the unborn (what she termed "the fetus-is-nothing paradigm of the pro-choice movement"), pro-choicers, she argued, were falling dangerously out of touch with the reality of abortion and women's experiences with it. In order to avert the loss of credibility and thus political influence the abortion movement would suffer thereby (although to her credit, Wolf also cited the need simply "to be faithful to the truth"), she asserted the "need to contextualize the fight to defend abortion rights within a moral framework that admits that the death of a fetus is a real death."

This remarkable essay is liable to engender, in the pro-life observer, the same kind of cognitive dissonance that "safe, legal, and rare" does. In it Wolf admits bluntly that the fetus is a live human being with a certain value and that abortion undoubtedly kills that human being. . . . She insists that abortion calls for a period of "mourning" and recommends spiritual "mending" ceremonies for women who abort, for vigils outside abortion clinics "commemorating and saying goodbye to the dead."

Yet her practical aim all along is to help other pro-abortionists develop a better strategy for keeping abortion legal.

Wolf avoids adopting conventional pro-life convictions by assigning the significance of the guilt and blood and killing to interior categories only. "If I found myself in circumstances in which I had to make the terrible decision to end this life," she writes, "then that would be between myself and God." For the unhappily pregnant woman, oppressed by patriarchal society and burdened by this fellow-victim inside her womb, abortion is not a social injustice but a personal "failure"; an evil to be borne and acknowledged and slowly atoned for.

For its frank admission (and thus diffusion) of the evidence that abortion kills a living human being, and its conclusion that this evidence doesn't logically require prohibition of abortion—and in fact may even lend its perpetrators a certain tragic nobility—Wolf's argument is a powerful one. Its effects live on in every pro-choice apologist who tries to imbue his position with moral gravity—or, as with our next case, in those who invoke the name of God.

Invoking God in Support of Abortion

Some abortion advocates pick up Wolf's ball and run even farther with it. For some, God might be not merely patiently tolerant, even sympathetic, toward this business of feticide; He may in fact positively endorse it, as the exercise of a mature and devout conscience. For sure, the landscape is dotted with liberal churches and associations of them, each self-defined as "pro-choice." But the biggest and best organizational representation of the religious pro-abortion folk can be found within the Religious Coalition for Reproductive Choice (RCRC), Planned Parenthood's collar-and-chasuble [priestly garment] lackey.

Beginning with the assertion that "most people of faith are pro-choice because of their religious beliefs, not in spite of them," the RCRC attempts to build a case for abortion on both sectarian and interreligious principles. First, compassion: "People who follow Jesus . . . should bring healing and wholeness to those in distress," claims one of the canned sermons the group offers as a resource. This means not forcing them into back alleys for their "healing" abortions and not forbidding them to opt out of the life-threatening ordeal of childbirth. Of course, there's good ol' freedom of conscience, too. Didn't Jesus "emphasize the moral agency of each person"? By this He compels us to believe that a woman's "life, health, and freedom . . . are more important than the potential life in her womb. . . ."

One could spend a great deal of time deconstructing the RCRC—its sophistic mastery of religious vocabulary and concepts; its historical place in the disintegration of American mainline Protestantism; its clever self-positioning as an "equal but opposite" voice in the abortion debate and thus its successful bid to neutralize the natural advantage the pro-life side enjoys in religious contexts.

But I will make just one other observation: *It's the pro-abortion side that always wants to turn this into a religious issue.* Sure, there's no shortage of biblical positivist pro-lifers, but by and large, the pro-life side would like to frame the debate in social-justice terms. One needn't be a Christian to oppose murder or to look at a sonogram. Conversely the pro-abortionists need desperately to paint the issue as a struggle against religious zealotry.

To these folks it is always an effective—and unexpected—rejoinder to ask that they stop talking about God so much.

> *"Jesus's teachings emphasized the religious freedom and moral agency of each person, male or female. Thus I believe that we are called by God to be active in the struggle to preserve and enhance reproductive choice for all people."*

Abortion Can Be Defended on Religious Grounds

Religious Coalition for Reproductive Choice

The Religious Coalition for Reproductive Choice (RCRC) is an organization of national religious organizations from all major religious faiths and traditions. Founded in 1973 to protect the newly won constitutional right to abortion from legal and political challenges, the organization describes itself as "pro-choice, not pro-abortion." It states further: "We do not at any time advocate for abortion but we do advocate for women and men making their own decisions about their reproductive life, in consultation with their faith tradition." The following viewpoint provides a more detailed explanation of the religious underpinnings of the RCRC's position on abortion.

Religious Coalition for Reproductive Choice, "A Sermon for Christian Congregations," *www.rcrc.org*, 2007. Reproduced by permission.

As you read, consider the following questions:

1. According to the author, when did American religious leaders first begin publicly speaking out for abortion rights?

2. Which amendment to the Constitution does the RCRC cite in support of its pro-choice position?

3. How does the RCRC use the example of Jesus's life and teachings to support its pro-choice orientation?

Some time ago, a woman called the Religious Coalition for Reproductive Choice, looking for pastoral counseling. She was 12 weeks pregnant, had a heart condition, was diabetic, and was now on bed rest. The doctor told her that the fetus probably would not make it to term, and there was a strong possibility that she might not, either. She had to make a decision about having an abortion within the week. An abortion any later would be dangerous for her, possibly life-threatening. She came to the Religious Coalition, asking for advice and counseling, and also wanting to know if God would ever forgive her if she "killed the baby."

Many, many women who consider abortion go through the same religious questioning and trauma that this woman experienced, sometimes supported by the love of their partners and family members but often without that support. Stories such as these are doubly tragic not only because of the terrible situations women find themselves in but also because women so often are unable to find comfort in their faith, instead seeing their faith as a source of fear, guilt, and rejection. They are too often unaware that their faith can be a source of comfort, love, compassion, and strength.

The Example of Jesus

The gospel narratives show Jesus as compassionate, forgiving and healing—especially to those in great distress. In the stories from the 5th chapter of Mark we see Jesus even willing to heal under duress, such as when a very ill woman startles him by touching his clothing. According to the laws and practices of the time, Jesus had every reason to ignore her, indeed to stay far away from her. Not only was she a woman, but she had been bleeding for 12 years, making her perpetually unclean. Unable to get control of her own health, she undoubtedly lived at the extreme margins of the society because everyone would be squeamish about having contact with her. Jesus had every right to reject her and rebuke her for what she did, but instead he called her "Daughter" and brought healing to both her body and her spirit. As people who follow Jesus, that's what we should be doing as well—bringing healing and wholeness to those in distress.

The Religious Right would like the American public to believe that to be religious is to be anti-choice. In reality, religious leaders worked toward legalizing abortion for years before *Roe v. Wade*. In the 60s, horrified by the injuries and death suffered by women around the country due to illegal, unsafe abortions, religious leaders responded as people of faith and conscience must. Reverend Howard Moody and Arlene Carmen organized the first Clergy Consultation Service in New York City, a network of clergy who agreed to help women gain access to safe abortion providers. Similar services soon developed throughout the country, and provided thousands of referrals for abortions that were necessary—but illegal—prior to the *Roe* decision.

Many Christians avoid thinking or talking about abortion because it makes them squeamish. But abortion is a topic that we must talk about from time to time, even in the church. And it is a topic that is directly related to freedom, especially religious freedom.

Abortion and Freedom of Religion

All of us, regardless of our denomination, have an interest in protecting the integrity of the First Amendment guarantee of freedom of religion, which says, "Congress shall make no law respecting an establishment of religion, or prohibiting the free exercise thereof." Without this guarantee, we would be in danger of losing a most fundamental human right, living out our faith only with the permission of whoever could gain official sanction for their religious views. And at the center of religious freedom is keeping the government out of personal moral decisions such as terminating a pregnancy.

I want to acknowledge that some Christians believe that life begins at conception and therefore abortion is wrong. They are entitled to that perspective, even though both the biblical basis and the historical basis for it are flimsy. However, having said that they are entitled to that view, we must also acknowledge that millions of Christians—indeed a majority of Protestants in this country—have a different view, believing instead that a fertilized egg is potential life but not actual life. These Christians hold that the life, health, freedom, and moral agency of the pregnant woman are more important than the potential life in her womb. The religious liberty that lies at the bedrock of our free society provides a basis for people with these competing beliefs to live together in one society, assured—we hope—that government will not choose sides.

On January 22, 2004, we observe the 31st anniversary of the landmark Supreme Court decision *Roe v Wade*, which made abortion legal in this country. And as we observe, we celebrate—not because abortion is terrific or wonderful, but because women have the ability to make health care decisions for themselves, and as a result, women's lives are saved.

According to fact sheets from Planned Parenthood and the Center for Reproductive Rights, in the pre-*Roe* year 1965, abortion was so unsafe that 17 percent of all deaths due to pregnancy and childbirth were the result of illegal abortion. It is estimated that illegal abortion led to between 5,000 and 10,000 deaths per year. Today, abortion is 11 times safer than

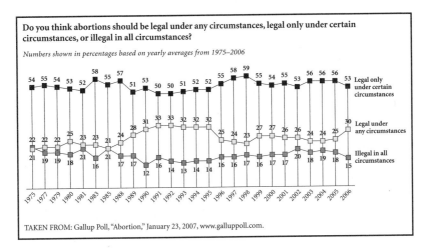

Do you think abortions should be legal under any circumstances, legal only under certain circumstances, or illegal in all circumstances?

Numbers shown in percentages based on yearly averages from 1975–2006

TAKEN FROM: Gallup Poll, "Abortion," January 23, 2007, www.galluppoll.com.

childbirth. Legal abortion has been associated with decreases in both maternal and infant mortality. According to one estimate, 1,500 pregnancy-related deaths were prevented in 1985 alone, because women were able to obtain abortions for difficult pregnancies.

A Step Toward Gender Equality

We also celebrate this anniversary because we embrace the value of full equality for women, and we recognize that true equality can only be fully realized if women have control over their own reproductive lives. Justice Harry Blackmun, who wrote the majority decision in *Roe*, recognized this. He called the decision "a step that had to be taken as we go down the road toward the full emancipation of women."

Unfortunately *Roe v. Wade* came under attack almost from the moment it was decided. Today, 31 years later, *Roe v. Wade* is still under attack and is in real danger of being overturned, or so seriously undermined as to be de facto [in fact] nonexistent. Largely due to the efforts of the Religious Right, *Roe v. Wade* has been compromised and diluted and currently hangs by a judicial thread.

The First Amendment guarantee of religious freedom was eroded by the Religious Right's efforts to have its narrow view of when life begins become the law of the land, as in the 1989 Supreme Court case, *Webster v. Reproductive Health Services.* This restrictive abortion law passed in Missouri contained in its preamble the statement that life begins at conception. The Supreme Court allowed that statement to stand in the preamble. Many religious, God-fearing people have a different view. Thus, the *Webster* decision struck at the very heart of the Constitutional guarantee regarding the separation of church and state, as it enshrined into law a religious belief held by some, but by no means all, Americans. Similar attempts by the Religious Right to enshrine in law their idea about the morality of abortion threaten to strip away once and for all our right to believe and practice our own faith.

Threats to Abortion Rights

Roe has been undermined in a host of different ways. In 1992, the Supreme Court decided, in *Planned Parenthood of Southeastern Pennsylvania v. Casey*, that states could impose restrictions on access to abortion, as long as these restrictions did not pose an "undue burden" on women's rights to reproductive freedom. This has opened the floodgates to all kinds of restrictive and even punitive laws, including waiting periods, so-called informed consent laws by which women are made to listen to false and misleading information on abortion that is designed to discourage them from making this choice, and parental consent and parental notification laws, designed to make it extremely difficult for a minor to obtain an abortion.

These are just some of the legal barriers placed on a woman's right to choose. The facts on the ground are in some ways even more disturbing. Today, 87 percent of counties in the United States have no abortion provider at all. And the population of doctors who are willing and trained to perform abortions is aging, with few young doctors being trained to take their places. Religious institutions are taking over public hospitals and HMOs and imposing their religious views on abortion, contraception, and sterilization on the general population whom the hospitals serve, often resulting in an end to these reproductive health services.

The latest, and in some ways most egregious, of the legal challenges to *Roe* is the so-called Partial Birth Abortion Ban, which President [George W.] Bush has signed into law and which is being challenged in the courts. The rhetoric surrounding the debate on this law would have us believe that thousands of women, up to the final moments of pregnancy, are deciding on a whim to terminate their pregnancies and are obtaining abortions. This caricature is nonsense. In fact, 88 percent of abortions occur in the first 12–13 weeks of pregnancy. According to the National Abortion Federation, "Women have access to abortion in the third trimester only in extreme circumstances. Fewer than 2 percent of abortions are performed 21 weeks or after, and they are extremely rare after 26 weeks of pregnancy, generally limited to cases of severe fetal abnormalities or situations when the life or health of the pregnant woman is seriously threatened."

In reality, this legislation arose from a deceptive and corrupt misinformation campaign to inflame the public, confuse the media, criminalize doctors, and strip women of their ability to make medical decisions. Thirty-one years after *Roe v. Wade*, it should be unthinkable that a doctor could be prosecuted as a criminal for performing an abortion procedure, yet that is what would happen under this bill. The absence of a health exception makes it clear that the purpose of this legislation is to undermine the legality of all abortions throughout pregnancy, not to outlaw some procedures.

In 2000, the Supreme Court struck down a similar bill in Nebraska, in the case known as *Stenberg v. Carhart.* The vote was 5–4. This 5–4 vote in *Stenberg* is an ominous sign for *Roe*'s future. The Supreme Court is only one vote away from overturning *Roe*, which would be one of the most radical actions taken in the history of the Court. Without *Roe*, life for

American women would be thrown more than 30 years in reverse, returning them to the days when women could not fully control the number and spacing of their children. Without *Roe*, women will be forced to carry fetuses to full term—even when those fetuses have no brain, no limbs, no heart.

Christian Responsibility

It is our responsibility as Christians who believe that God has given freedom to all of us—including women—to do all in our power to keep *Roe* as the law of the land. You may not choose to have an abortion yourself, but the right of women to obtain an abortion when needed is a right you should care about strongly. We must speak out, we must vote, we must march, picket and protest. We must let our lawmakers know that we will not allow them to take us back to the days of back-alley abortions that threaten women's health and even their very lives.

Abortion is a difficult subject, but it does not arise in a vacuum, and we should never try to think about it in a vacuum. How we think about abortion is inextricably linked to the core values of our faith. Jesus' life among us demonstrated God's compassion and love for every person, as well as God's deep desire for justice and health to prevail. Jesus' teachings emphasized the religious freedom and moral agency of each person, male or female. Thus I believe that we are called by God to be active in the struggle to preserve and enhance reproductive choice for all people. As Christians who strive to follow Jesus, we can and must be both compassionate and pro-choice.

> *"I have always seen the decision not to terminate my pregnancy as the one courageous moment of my life. . . . But lately, I've begun to think it curious that I should have seen not killing my own child as heroic."*

Abortion Should Be Condemned on Religious Grounds

Christine A. Scheller

In this viewpoint, Christine A. Scheller, a religious writer based in southern California who regularly contributes to the evangelical magazine Christianity Today, *recalls her own decisionmaking process when she faced an unplanned pregnancy. Like many other people of faith who oppose abortion, she concludes that the pro-choice movement is based on a materialistic and selfish worldview. She also asserts that abortion is a clear moral wrong and that all of the rhetoric about the importance of "choice" and "reproductive freedom" is really just a disguise for avoiding responsibility for one's actions.*

Christine A. Scheller, "A Laughing Child in Exchange for Sin: What Exactly Does Courage Look Like in an Age of Abortion?" *Christianity Today*, vol. 48, February 2004, pp. 54–57. Reproduced by permission of the author.

As you read, consider the following questions:

1. What is the author's opinion of Kate Michelman, the former president of NARAL Pro-Choice America?

2. How did the author's non-Christian friends respond to her decision to reject abortion?

3. What point is the author making with her use of the scriptural lesson in Psalm 106:13–15?

Exchanging palm trees for stately oaks, I deposited my first-born child at a respected evangelical college this summer. It was an outcome nestled in the farthest reaches of my imagination when I was a pregnant college student 20 years ago. Dark, hopeless thoughts assaulted me throughout that pregnancy. I envisioned myself impoverished and alone or, in rare sunnier moments, as a bohemian heroine of sorts, dragging my grateful child along on my adventures. Still, I decided to keep my biracial baby after the counselor at the home for un-wed mothers advised me to put him up for adoption. She said, "You're going to marry a doctor or lawyer someday, and what will his friends think?"

Though I was completely inadequate to the task before me, I didn't ever want my child to think I had given him up for adoption because of the color of his skin. So I determined to become the parent he deserved.

When he was a month old, I was accepted, at my interview, into Moore College of Art and Design in Philadelphia. As the admissions officer urged me never to stop painting, I glimpsed my mother across the street walking the baby in the stroller, and I knew instinctively that I didn't have it in me to both be a mother and pursue a dream in a distant city. These experiences were the seedbed of authentic faith as I began to surrender to love.

A Loving Partner

Not long after, an unlikely prince rode into our lives. I find it nearly impossible to separate the Lord's redemptive work from my husband's powerful love. He didn't make the mess, but he also didn't shrink from entering into the fray the way some men do—those who, despite their own sins, run from the consequences inflicted upon the women and children they leave. His lavish devotion ministered healing year after year until the past largely disappeared. With my mother's help and his support, I earned a bachelor's degree a dozen years after leaving Eastern Mennonite University.

And yet the scar is still there. When my black son explains his white brother to his college dorm mates, it's with the shorthand, "Same mom; different dads." A perfect introduction to another generation's world of woe, and to my family's experience of periodically having my 20-year-old sin laid bare before strangers. The shorthand makes such moments easier for my children as surely as it inflicts a deep lash into both their parents. But as they remind us, they can't pretend our history isn't what it is. In some ways that's a blessing; it forces us out of the shadows.

I have always seen the decision not to terminate my pregnancy as the one courageous moment of my life. I acted with self-abandon for the benefit of the innocent. But lately, I've begun to think it curious that I should have seen not killing my own child as heroic. I could spin a sad tale to make myself look better, but the fact is I failed in my duty to my family, my community, and my Savior. Accepting the consequences of that failure was not heroism. Only in a culture where sex is divorced from meaning and where self-interest trumps everything could such a narrative be produced. Courage would have been to decline that offer of illicit comfort in the first place.

William Blake said of moral insurrectionists, "Mock on, mock on Voltaire, Rousseau; Mock on, mock on: 'tis all in

The Moral Evil of *Roe v. Wade*

"Choice" is a positive concept, and an attractive concept. That's why abortion apologists use it. But the way they use it is a lie and, increasingly, Americans are catching on. There is hope in this development.

There is also hope in the growing popular recognition that the decisions of the Supreme Court can be changed. The assertion of the Supreme Court in its Dred Scott decision (that slaves are not citizens), in time, was changed. The argument of the Court in its "separate-but-equal" *Plessy v. Ferguson* decision, in time, was changed. In each of these cases moral outrage was a decisive factor in the change. So it will be in the case of *Roe v. Wade*.

Increasingly, Americans are recognizing what a moral evil is embodied in *Roe*. Increasingly, they are aware of the vast network of lies that have been spun and fortified to sustain the illusion that abortion is somehow a good, or at least a morally neutral procedure; that it is a standard part of health care and family planning; that it is a proper exercise of a woman's freedom; that it is a solution to intractable social problems. It is, of course, none of these things. What it is, is an unfettered right to take an innocent human life from the mother's womb. All this, more and more Americans are coming to know.

William H. Keeler, Remarks delivered at Basilica of the National Shrine of the Immaculate Conception, reprinted in "The Blood of Innocents Continues to Stain Our Constitution," National Right to Life News, *February 2005.*

vain! You throw the sand against the wind, and the wind blows it back again." Perhaps my foolishness can be traced back to their brood, but I sometimes wonder when the baby boomers who sold me such a wretched bill of goods will at least sweep up the sand.

Maybe they didn't realize they were devouring their own children when they threw off the bonds of traditional morality, but they seem almost oblivious to the depths of their failure. The tired message of women like Kate Michelman, retiring president of NARAL Pro-Choice America, is part of their legacy.

Condemning the NARAL Message

The *New York Times* calls Michelman "one of the grand dames of the reproductive rights debate." She became an abortion activist after her husband abandoned the family when she was pregnant with their fourth child. She was humiliated to discover that she would need his permission and that of an all-male hospital board to obtain a legal abortion. (Imagine allowing a single humiliation to define you.) Michelman is stepping down to care for her ailing husband and their daughter, according to *The Times*. She says, "After nearly 20 years of pouring my heart and soul into this organization I must now put them first." It's an ironic statement from the lips of someone who advocated a utilitarian view of family for so many years.

Michelman says the "true impact" of NARAL can be measured by the "countless women whose lives have been saved and children whose lives have been enriched by our work." Though the lie is smooth as silk, her message is both hopeless and materialistic: hopeless because it says the human spirit cannot overcome devastation (in this case, of unwanted pregnancy), and materialistic because it assigns a family's economic concerns ultimate priority, devaluing the poor—not to mention the unborn—in the process.

My grandmother's experience makes Michelman's (and my own) look like a day at the beach. Abandoned by her husband in the slums of Newark, New Jersey, she raised seven children by herself. Then she raised three of her grandchildren after they too were abandoned. It could be said that this course of action led to an early grave, and she was not a happy woman toward the end of her life. But would any of my cousins or I say one of our parents should have been sacrificed in utero so the others could have had a better life—or so that our grandmother could have? I don't think so. We would all agree, however, that our grandfather should have been wrangled back from his real-estate pursuits in Florida and sentenced to forced labor for their support. My grandmother surrendered her life for her family. That's everyday nobility. It degrades us to sacrifice our children and call it virtue.

Michelman is obviously a resourceful woman. Somehow I think she would have managed to succeed, even with that fourth child. To say others are incapable of the same is nothing more than condescension. And it hardly seems necessary to mention that legalized abortion exponentially reinforces the male tendency toward sexual irresponsibility. The argument that legalizing abortion prevents back-alley abortion tragedies is like saying society ought to dance with the devil because unless we do, those who sleep with him might get torched.

A Worthy Legacy

Two boomer friends of mine provided a sharp contrast to Michelman and her peers. In addition to hosting an annual National Day of Prayer gathering at their expansive home, Jean Peterson ministered to unwed mothers and post-abortive women, while her husband Don counseled repentant substance abusers and financial mismanagers. They went about the work of redeeming a generation of Americans, all the while tethering that work to its source in prayer. They left this world as part of the group of passengers who saved our nation's capital from becoming the third target of terrorists on September 11, 2001. Theirs is the legacy worth emulating.

Oswald Chambers said, "God does not make us holy in the sense of character; he makes us holy in the sense of innocence, and we have to turn that innocence into holy character by a series of moral choices." It was more than I could grasp that Christ would render me innocent of my sin, but then without ever trying, I gained an unexpected moral authority among my non-Christian friends and acquaintances because of the choices I made after I sinned.

Their snickering at my pregnancy and early marriage gradually turned to respect. They would sometimes tell me that when they had moral decisions to make, they would consider what my husband or I might do. Women who had had abortions occasionally reinforced the idea that I had been courageous, particularly white middle class women with education, a group highly represented in abortion statistics.

Women like these identify with my moral failure, and that makes me non-threatening. But they also recognize the hope of redemption and the power of moral absolutes in a world that tells us neither is necessary. That I should gain moral authority after sin is about as mind-boggling as reconciling the sovereignty of God in my son's conception with that same sin. Nonetheless, it is a privileged witness to possess.

Pondering a Different Choice

There is a contrasting Christian witness, though. I write about it only because in our churches we so often talk about abortion as if it were an evil separate from us. But unless we are honest with ourselves about who we are, we cannot hope to turn our own culture on its head, let alone influence the larger one. One story suffices to describe it: My husband and I befriended a young woman years ago when he was a student at Philadelphia Biblical University. I was ripe with my second pregnancy when she abruptly disappeared from our lives. Several months later she reappeared with an explanation. She had had successive sexual relationships with two Bible college students. She had gotten pregnant by a youth leader of a Presbyterian church. He had driven her to the abortion clinic, paid to get rid of the problem—wouldn't even go inside with her—

then dropped her off at her dorm when it was over. She said she thought I would understand, and she knew God would forgive her. She continued serving in various ministries, graduated with her class, and married into a respected Christian family.

I attended her bridal shower, but I didn't "understand" for some time. I was angry at the perceived injustice of others "getting away with" their sin while mine was costly and public. The anger subsided and I began to feel sorry for her as I recalled my exquisite experience of the grace of God: A laughing child in exchange for sin. How incomparable! Those who pile sin on top of sin acquire instead the leanness of soul described in Psalm 106:13–15: "They soon forgot his works; they did not wait for his counsel, but lusted exceedingly in the wilderness, and tested God in the desert. And he gave them their request, but sent leanness into their soul." Think of David during his long-delayed repentance. I've heard it said that he never regained his moral authority because of his shame, thereby sowing destruction into his kingdom. I wonder how many Christians, because of shame over some act of duplicitous cover-up, are unable to speak with voices of moral certitude. And what is it costing our nation?

Using Failure to Strengthen Faith

There was an important distinction between me and the Bible college coed who had an abortion. When I discovered I was pregnant, I knew that, in spite their devastation at my betrayal, my parents loved me more than they cared what the neighbors thought. She didn't know any such thing; her Christian parents had scorned girls like me.

So if there was any hint of courage in my decision to abandon myself to motherhood prematurely, it was this: the exchange of the therapeutic shadow of a faith for an orthodox one. Or, as Puritan writer William Gurnall says in *The Christian in Complete Armour*, "God can, in fact, use his saints' failures to strengthen their faith, which, like a tree, stands stronger for the shaking. . . And here is all the devil gets: Instead of destroying the saint's faith, he is the means of refining it, thereby making it stronger and more precious."

How the next generation needs us to snatch back the victory from the enemy with faith that first rises valiantly from the failures of our own and then speaks with a sturdy voice. The narrative we transfer has to include our own repentance and it has to be more penetrating than the one I heard.

Twenty years of crafting a new narrative for my children came to a close on the lawn of a college much like the one where the sensate tale failed me. So hugging my son one last time before flying back to the palm trees, I left him with an exhortation: "Don't defraud anyone sexually, for God is the defender of all such."

Wryly he answered, "Can't a girl defraud me?"

"Yes," I conceded with a sigh, resisting the temptation to add, "But remember your mother, remember the pain she caused you, and let the wind take the sand far from you."

Periodical Bibliography

The following articles have been selected to supplement the diverse views presented in this chapter.

Erika Bachiochi   "How Abortion Hurts Women: The Hard Proof," *Crisis Magazine Online*, June 2005, www.crisismagazine.com.

Judith A. Baer   "Women's Rights and the Constitution," *Social Science Journal*, vol. 44, no. 1, 2007.

Sam Brownback   "Abortion and the Conscience of the Nation Revisited," *Human Life Review*, Summer 2004.

E.J. Dionne   "A Thorn in Both Their Sides," *Sojourners*, June 2006.

Howard Fineman   "The GOP's Abortion Anxiety," *Newsweek*, March 20, 2006.

Josh Harkinson   "Born-Again Abortion Clinics," *Mother Jones*, March–April 2007.

Charles I. Lugosi   "When Abortion Was a Crime: A Historical Perspective," *University of Detroit Mercy Law Review*, Winter 2006.

Mary Ellen Neill   "The Continued Betrayal of Women: U.S. Culture Exhorts Them to Be Sexual, but Not Pregnant," *National Catholic Reporter*, April 21, 2006.

Cristina Paige   "Contraception Saves Money and Marriages," *AlterNet*, December 21, 2006, www.alternet.org.

Lois M. Powell and Ann L. Hansen   "The Reality of Legalized Abortion: People of Faith Support a Woman's Right to Choose," *United Church of Christ Online*, www.uccc.org.

Donna Schaper   "My Choice," *Tikkun*, July–August 2006.

OPPOSING
VIEWPOINTS®
SERIES

CHAPTER 4

What Issues of Sexuality Surround Religious Leaders?

Chapter Preface

In the last two decades of the twentieth century, the sexuality of religious leaders has emerged as a leading topic of discussion and study in religious denominations within a wide range of faiths. Various religious institutions and groups are devoting greater attention to the ways in which the sexual activities and beliefs of clergy influence the health and vitality of congregations. This increased attention is due in part to high-profile sex scandals that have profoundly embarrassed some religious groups. But the heightened attention also stems in part from growing recognition of the terrible damage that clergy sexual misconduct can do to churches—and in part from heightened awareness of the unique social pressures that pastors, rabbis, and other church leaders deal with on a regular basis.

This increased attention to clergy sexuality has turned up some interesting data. A 2005 "sex and the church" survey conducted by Christianity Today International, for example, revealed that pastors are much more likely to be happily married than laity, in some measure because of higher levels of satisfaction with their sex lives. But seven out of ten pastors also reported that they had been propositioned to engage in romantic or sexual activity by non-spouses at some point in their career—and nearly one in ten stated that they had to ward off these advances from parishioners or other community members on a regular (more than once a year) basis. Finally, 5 percent of the pastors in the survey confessed to having committed adultery at least once since becoming a pastor.

Other issues of clergy sexuality have also assumed new prominence in recent years. After enduring an onslaught of sex-abuse scandals involving priests, members of the Catholic Church are debating the Vatican's ban on married or female priests with ever greater vigor. Leaders and members of the

Catholic faith are also joining Anglican, Protestant, Jewish, and other religious denominations in spirited debates about the moral and scriptural appropriateness of placing women and homosexuals in church leadership positions. The following viewpoints provide contrasting assessments of some of these issues, but they all reflect a conviction that these issues will dictate the future of U.S. religion and religious faith for generations to come.

> *"The truth of the nonultimacy of sex, family, and worldly relationship can and should be proclaimed through words, but it will be believed only when people can see it."*

Rules of Celibacy Should Be Supported

Robert Barron

In the following viewpoint, Father Robert Barron strongly affirms traditional Catholic rules of celibacy for members of the priesthood. A professor of systematic theology at Mundelein Seminary outside Chicago, Illinois, Barron believes that priestly celibacy is a vital tool in showing Catholic people of faith about the "transcendant form of love" that awaits believers in heaven. He claims that the example of celibate priests is often an inspiration to Catholic worshippers.

As you read, consider the following questions:

1. What does the author think about arguments that sexual contact within marriage would render priests "impure"?

2. What parallels does Barron draw between the sacrament of the Eucharist and priestly celibacy?

Robert Barron, "Why Celibacy Makes Sense," *Commonweal*, August 12, 2005, pp. 17–19. Copyright © 2005 Commonweal Publishing Co., Inc. Reproduced by permission of Commonweal Foundation.

3. Does Barron admit to any personal struggles with celibacy?

There is a very bad argument for celibacy that has appeared from time to time throughout the tradition and is, even today [2005], defended by some. It runs something like this: married life is morally and spiritually suspect; priests, as religious leaders, should be spiritual athletes above reproach; therefore, priests shouldn't be married. I love Augustine [an early Catholic saint], but it's hard to deny that this argument finds support in some of his more unfortunate reflections on sexuality (original sin as a sexually transmitted disease; sex even within marriage is venially sinful; the birth of a baby associated with excretion, etc.). I ran across a recent book in which the author presented a version of this justification, appealing to the purity codes in the book of Leviticus. His implication was that any sort of sexual contact, even within marriage, would render a minister at the altar impure. This approach to the question is not just silly but dangerous, for it rests on assumptions that are repugnant to good Christian metaphysics. . . .

According to the biblical narratives, when God wanted to make a certain truth vividly known to his people, he would, at times, choose a prophet and command him to act out that truth. So, he told Hosea to marry the unfaithful Gomer in order to sacramentalize God's fidelity to wavering Israel. In *The Grammar of Assent*, John Henry Newman reminds us that truth is brought home to the mind when it is represented, not through abstractions, but through something particular, colorful, imaginable. Thus, the truth of the nonultimacy of sex, family, and worldly relationship can and should be proclaimed through words, but it will be believed only when people can see it.

This is why, the church is convinced, God chooses certain people to be celibate in order to witness to a transcendent form of love, the way that we will love in heaven. In God's

Celibacy Symbolizes the Priest's Special Bond with Christ

Above all, the priesthood in the New Testament is a participation in the Priesthood of Our Lord Jesus Christ, the High Priest. And, therefore, the priest has a mysterious and special bond with Christ, in whose name and by whose power he offers the bloodless sacrifice (*in persona Christi*). The most profound reason for priestly celibacy comes from this supernatural bond with the Savior.

Luiz Sérgio Solimeo. "Tracing the Glorious Origins of Celibacy,"
American Society for the Defense of Tradition, Family, and Property,
www.tfp.org.

realm, we will experience a communion (bodily as well as spiritual) more intense than even the most intense forms of communion here below, and celibates make this truth viscerally real for us now. Just as belief in the Real Presence in the Eucharist fades when unaccompanied by devotional practice, so the belief in the impermanence of created love becomes attenuated in the absence of living embodiments of it. Though one can present practical reasons for it, I believe that celibacy only finally makes sense in this eschatological context.

The Priesthood as a Eucharistic Vocation

I realize that you might be following the argument to this point and still feel compelled to ask, "Yes, granted that celibacy is a good thing for the church, but why must all priests be celibate?" The medievals distinguished between arguments from necessity and arguments from "fittingness." I can offer only the latter kind of argument, for even its most ardent defenders admit that celibacy is not essential to the priesthood. After all, married priests have been, at various times and for various reasons, accepted from the beginning of the church to the present day. The appropriateness of linking priesthood and celibacy comes, I think, from the priest's identity as a eucharistic person. All that a priest is radiates from his unique capacity, acting in the person of Christ, to transform the eucharistic elements into the body and blood of Jesus. As the center of a rose window anchors and orders all the other elements in the design, so the eucharistic act of the priest grounds and animates everything else that he does, rendering qualitatively distinctive his way of leading, sanctifying, and teaching. The Eucharist is the eschatological act par excellence, for as Paul says, "every time we eat this bread and drink this cup, we proclaim the death of the Lord until he comes." To proclaim the Paschal Mystery [Jesus Christ's mission of salvation] through the Eucharist is to make present that event by which the new world is opened up to us. It is to make vividly real the transcendent dimension that effectively relativizes (without denying) all the goods of this passing world. And it is therefore fitting that the one who is so intimately conditioned by and related to the Eucharist should be in his form of life an eschatological person.

For years, Andrew Greeley has been arguing—quite rightly—that the priest is fascinating and that a large part of the fascination comes from celibacy. The compelling quality of the priest is not a matter of superficial celebrity or charm; that gets us nowhere. It is something much stranger, deeper, more mystical. It is the fascination for another world, for that mysterious dimension of existence hinted at by the universe here below and revealed to us in the breaking of the bread. I for one am glad that such eschatologically fascinating persons are not simply in monasteries, cloistered convents, and hermits' cells, but in parishes, on the streets, in the pulpits, moving among the people of God.

Struggling with Celibacy

There are, I realize, a couple of major problems with offering arguments for celibacy. First, it can make everything seem so pat, rational, and resolved. I've been a priest for nearly twenty years, and I can assure you that the living of celibacy has been anything but that. As I've gone through different seasons of my life as a priest, I've struggled mightily with celibacy, precisely because the tension between the goodness and ephemerality of creation that I spoke of earlier is no abstraction; rather it runs right through my body. The second problem is that reason goes only so far. As Thomas More said to his daughter in *A Man for All Seasons*, as he was trying to explain why he was being so stubborn: "Finally, Meg, it's not a matter of reason; finally, it's a matter of love."

People in love do strange things: they pledge eternal fidelity; they write poetry and songs; they defy their families and change their life plans; sometimes they go to their deaths. They tend to be over the top, irrational, confounding to the reasonable people around them. Though we can make a case for it—as I have tried to do—celibacy is finally inexplicable, unnatural, fascinating, for it is a form of life adopted by people in love with Jesus Christ.

> *"No doubt there are many great and holy bishops and priests. But we all lack in one basic area—a lived experience of married love. All the good will in the world doesn't make up for this lack of experience."*

Rules of Celibacy Should Be Abandoned

Alan Phillip

Within today's Roman Catholic Church, a great debate has arisen among leaders and laity about rules of celibacy in the priesthood. In the following article, Father Alan Phillip, a Catholic priest at the Mater Dolorosa Passionist Retreat Center in Sierra Madre, California, urges the Church to discard its celibacy rules. He asserts that longstanding rules forbidding Catholic priests from marrying deprive them of the "human wholeness and spiritual holiness" that can be achieved through the sacrament of marriage. Phillip also stresses that forced celibacy limits priests' ability to provide helpful spiritual guidance to congregants in matters of sex and marriage.

Alan Phillip. "How Father Can Know Best." *U.S. Catholic*, vol. 69, July 1, 2004, pp. 24–28. Copyright © 2004 by Claretian Publications. Reproduced by permission.

As you read, consider the following questions:

1. According to Phillip, what are some of the ways in which modern society shows its anxiety and preoccupation with sex?

2. How do Catholic congregations view the counsel of priests in the areas of sex and marriage, according to Phillip?

3. Which scriptural passages does Phillip rely on to support his arguments?

Last-year's letters to the U.S. bishops from priests in several dioceses brought the issue of optional celibacy into the headlines again. The priests' letters highlighted the serious shortage of priests and the growing lack of available eucharistic celebration for the faithful.

I agree with the contents of the letters. But there is a broader and equally serious reason that needs to be raised.

These days we humans are having real difficulties with our sexuality. A brief glance at TV, the movies, the Internet, and the local magazine rack gives a quick sampling of our unbalance. Advertisers use sex to sell products. Singers use sex to mask their lack of musical talent. Talk shows are obsessed with sexual aberrations.

Considering the extent of prostitution, adultery, group sex, pedophilia, and spousal abuse, one must conclude that our society hasn't got a clue about why we were created male and female.

For much of our society, sex is seen as something people use for entertainment, for selling products, or for manipulating others. The problem is not just sexual aberration and exploitation. The real offense against human sexuality is that it is trivialized.

Many people experience sex as something that is pleasurable but devoid of meaning. Sex for them becomes a shallow activity, intensely involving the body but offering little con-

nection to the soul. Their sexual encounters engage physical organs but not the person. They settle for sex appeal, when what is possible is self-realization. They settle for technique, when what is possible is transcendence.

Very simply, what was designed to reach the very core of the human soul has been relegated to the surface. What was meant to free people from their egos has instead entrapped them in the realm of self-centeredness. There is no commitment. There is no trust. There is no love.

In the midst of this mess, to whom can we turn for help?

Finding Spiritual Guidance

Logically, people should turn to their ordained spiritual leaders for guidance. Ah, here is the problem for Catholics. A medieval law still in force in our Roman Catholic community requires all bishops and priests to be celibate. No doubt there are many great and holy bishops and priests. But we all lack in one basic area—a lived experience of married love.

All the good will in the world doesn't make up for this lack of experience. As spiritual leaders we priests haven't "walked a mile in the shoes" of the married people we are meant to lead. We are lacking the sexual experience that is possible within marriage. We can preach about the shoulds and should nots of sexual morality. And we can certainly say a lot about abstinence, denial, and sublimation. But what do we know of the human wholeness and spiritual holiness that can be achieved in the bonding of body, heart, will, and soul through the sacrament of Marriage?

Our world, perhaps more than ever before, is in critical need of a healthy vision of human sexuality. Young people especially need believable pacesetters in sexual maturity. The church needs to proclaim from the rooftops that it has a better message about sex than the culture offers. We priests, who are the most visible wisdom figures, who are ordained to be teachers and sages, need among our number those who will give prophetic witness to the goodness and beauty of married love.

Approach married couples in a typical Catholic parish and ask them: "When was the last time you heard a Sunday homily about married spirituality?" Most likely, they will scratch their heads, think for awhile, and then respond, "Maybe once last year," or "Along time ago," or even, "Never."

Most of the people in our pews are either married, have been married, or will one day be married. They live much of their life practicing their faith and finding their path to holiness through the sacrament of Marriage. They could certainly use some guidance, direction, and even leadership in their holy vocation.

Unfortunately, they cannot get much help from priests because we are all celibate. Let's be honest. In the eyes of the faithful, we are very limited in what we can preach. Our homilies and other teachings are narrowed to life as seen through the eyes of a celibate.

The result? At best, there is a vast population of married people floundering about with sparse spiritual direction for a major segment of their lives. Many turn to other churches where a married clergy understands their experience and speaks their language. At worst, there are dysfunctional families, a high divorce rate, spousal abuse, and a large array of other problems that are compounded when there is no effective conjugal leadership from our pulpits.

Need for Change

The first moral statement in the Bible proclaims, "It is not good for the man to be alone." Where do we find the church proclaiming by word and example the goodness of God's plan for sexuality? Where does our ordained leadership witness to communion with the Creator through communion with one's spouse?

The Catholic Church needs to give clear spiritual direction, by word and the example of its spiritual leaders, that will guide married couples on their sacramental journey to God.

The Catholic Church needs to promote respect for the human body, teaching by word and the example of its spiritual leaders, the dignity, nobility, and sanctity of human sexuality.

The Catholic Church needs to proclaim to our youth, by word and the example of its spiritual leaders, the power of premarital and marital chastity to shape the human heart for a trust-filled and lifelong union.

The Catholic Church, in stating its position on homosexuality, needs to show, by word and the example of its spiritual leaders, what it truly believes about marriage between a man and woman.

In responding to the crisis of pedophilia, the Catholic Church needs to do more than apologize with words. It needs to declare by the example of its spiritual leaders what a wholesome relationship with children is like, especially in family life.

To fulfill this mission is the urgent challenge before our church today. In the early days of his pontificate, Pope John Paul II wrote eloquently about the "theology of the body." But words alone are not enough. It is time for visible witness. It was St. Francis who advised his followers, "Preach the gospel at all times. If necessary, use words." He knew that people learn by observing.

Our world needs no more words, words, words. It longs for leaders to show us by the power of example what the Creator intended in creating sexual beings. A return to our apostolic roots by opening up ministry to a married clergy would be an eloquent profession of faith by our church that married couples are called to holiness of life.

It would make no more sense to mandate that priests marry than it makes to mandate celibacy. The vocation of marriage should not be imposed but should be a response to a call from the Lord. In view of the reasons above, now would be the perfect time to bring back to active ministry all those ordained who went on to answer a further call to married life.

Reexamine Assumptions

It is not difficult to find people who have the courage of their convictions. What is rare to find are people who have the courage to reexamine their convictions. St. Peter, the first pope, had this second brand of courage. He went through much of his life regarding gentiles as unclean. He thought they were unworthy of his association. This was part of his tradition.

But new circumstances (and a dream) forced Peter to reexamine his convictions. And he came to a new conclusion. "I begin to see how true it is that God shows no partiality" (Acts 10:34). This was such a significant change for Peter that Luke relates it twice in the Acts of the Apostles.

I pray that our American bishops will somehow find the courage to reexamine their convictions. They are being asked to reexamine if they "teach as dogma mere human precepts" (Mark 7:7).

Then, inspired by the bravery of our American bishops, I trust that the next pope will have the courage to reexamine the church's rule requiring celibacy for all priests. Yes, it will take courage to change. But 21st-century pastoral needs cannot be answered with an 11th-century law. A law of mandatory celibacy is powerless to reverse the mentality of our present culture's sexual sickness. It is time for a change.

I believe a new Pentecost for the Catholic Church will soon be realized and a renewed excitement about human sexuality in the context of conjugal love will soon be experienced. Just imagine a time when words preached from the pulpit are spoken in a language and mirrored by an example once again understood by married couples—and young people on the way to marriage.

"[Clergywomen have] brought new perspectives into the theological discussion, a more inclusive style, and opened the doors to worshippers who've felt disengaged from institutional religion."

The Ordination of Women Is a Positive Development in Religious Communities

Jane Lampman

Although a number of large Christian, Jewish, Muslim, and other religious denominations in the United States remain officially opposed to having women as clergy, many other Christian and Jewish denominations have embraced clergywomen. As this viewpoint details, the growth in women clergy in these denominations has been seen overwhelmingly as a positive development. Clergywomen have been credited with revitalizing church communities, bringing fresh perspectives to religious and social outreach efforts, and creating a more welcoming environment for worshippers. Jane Lampman is a staff writer for the Christian Science Monitor.

Jane Lampman, "Women Clergy Bring a New Sensibility to an Old Calling," *Christian Science Monitor*, July 19, 2006. Copyright © 2006 The Christian Science Publishing Society. All rights reserved. Reproduced by permission from *Christian Science Monitor,* (www.csmonitor.com).

As you read, consider the following questions:

1. In which major Christian denomination do clergy-women comprise the majority of the denomination's clergy?
2. According to the author, what percentage of seminary students in 2006 are women?
3. In what ways are women rabbis influencing Jewish worship practices and beliefs?

The "stained-glass ceiling" was breached in dramatic fashion this summer, when bishops of the US Episcopal Church unexpectedly elected Katharine Jefferts Schori to be the church's leader for the next nine years.

Yet that glass ceiling remains relatively intact, even though the ranks of women clergy and their impact on religious communities continue to grow. It's perhaps no surprise that women's leadership remains controversial, since the two largest Christian denominations in the US—Roman Catholics and Southern Baptists—reject women as pastors. So do Eastern Orthodox, Mormons, some Evangelicals, Muslims, and Orthodox Jews.

Still, thousands of clergywomen are filling rewarding and increasingly influential roles as ministers, priests, bishops, and rabbis. And it's not the numbers or even the level of acceptance that's at the heart of the issue, many say—it's a divine calling.

"God called me, and I have such a sense of that, that it's the defining thing," says the Rev. Nancy Rankin, twice a senior pastor and now director of congregational development for the United Methodist Church (UMC) in western North Carolina.

Growing Ranks of Women Clergy

The UMC and the Presbyterian Church (USA) are currently [in 2006] celebrating 50 years of ordaining women. The Methodists boast some 12,000 clergywomen; and 20 percent of Presbyterian clergy are female. Unitarian Universalists stand out as the one denomination to have a majority of women leaders.

Some Christian and Jewish clergywomen with years of experience—and who've reached the challenging and often-elusive post of senior pastor—say they still encounter resistance. They point to frontiers that remain, but are also encouraged by the strides already made.

"I wanted to be a rabbi long before women could, but I didn't think it would happen in my lifetime," says Rabbi Susan Grossman, who leads Beth Shalom, a Conservative Jewish congregation in Columbia, Md. "There's been more change in women's role in Judaism in the last 30 years than probably all of Jewish history!"

Women of both faiths share the experiences of difficulty in finding jobs, being shunted into smaller, often remote congregations, and receiving lower pay and fewer benefits than their male counterparts, as shown by studies of both Protestant clergy and Conservative Jewish rabbis.

Partly out of necessity and partly out of inclination, women have extended the boundaries of ministry beyond the congregation to serve as both military and hospital chaplains, educators, and counselors for social service agencies, according to a major 1998 study, "Clergy Women: An Uphill Calling."

Trials and Triumphs

Studies also show that clergywomen experience more stress than their male counterparts in a demanding occupation. As a result, a number are leaving the pulpit.

At the same time, clergywomen have been credited with being less interested in hierarchy and more in collegiality. They've brought new perspectives into the theological discus-

Praise for a Female Priest

Janet [the chaplain at the University of Minnesota's Episcopal Center, who has been a priest for ten years] is a priest who does not put on airs. She does not make a point of calling attention to her status by the use of either titles or clerical garb. She is not churchy. She's a natural. Watching her is like watching the seals at the Oregon coast. You know she belongs exactly where she is.

I am sure that God watches Janet with both thumbs up and a big grin, well pleased with this beloved daughter. Otherwise her work would seem disordered or strained, her presence not so life-giving, her ministry less fruitful. In vain would the builder labor.

Anne Marie Wolf, "She's a Natural,"
Commonweal, January 14, 2005.

sion, a more inclusive style, and opened the doors to worshippers who've felt disengaged from institutional religion.

"My mother often said that if there had been women rabbis when she was young, she wouldn't have been alienated from Judaism," says Ms. Grossman.

The role models clergywomen provide are spurring other young women to enter seminaries, where today they make up between 30 and 50 percent of students. "I grew up not ever seeing women in ministry. ... The girls in this congregation don't think twice about it," says the Rev. Shannon Kershner, senior pastor at Woodhaven Presbyterian Church in Irving, Texas.

Despite the numerous challenges, many women find the profession immensely satisfying and an opportunity to influence their faith communities.

A Woman Rabbi Looks Back

Grossman was in the first class of ordained Conservative rabbis in 1985 and has been in the pulpit for 17 years. She's in an elite class of women who've become senior rabbis leading large congregations.

What means most to her, she says, is bringing comfort and support to people at meaningful moments in their lives. She also prizes "being able to mobilize the community for interfaith work, for peace work, for countering domestic violence. It's tremendously satisfying to do that authentically as a Jewish leader," she says.

And a leader she has become in the Jewish community. Grossman has served as an editor of the Conservative commentary on Scripture (Torah) and as a member of a committee on Jewish law and standards, which enables her to help make Jewish law "more woman-friendly." Her "rabbinic decision" on women serving as witnesses in Jewish law is now an official Conservative position.

Still, even when she took up her latest position, some people left the synagogue because she was a woman. While the difficulties over the years have led her to consider leaving the job several times, "I'm so glad I stuck it out, because now I'm thrilled with the pulpit," she adds.

Jaqueline Ellenson, director of the Women's Rabbinic Network in the Reform Jewish movement, also points to progress. The more liberal Reform denomination was the first, in 1972, to ordain a woman rabbi—the recently retired Sally Priesand. Now 450 women constitute about a quarter of the 1,800 Reform rabbis.

"The walls are down in terms of attitudes toward women rabbis in the movement—getting jobs is no longer an issue," she says. But other challenges remain, particularly bringing about pay and benefit equity. "And women are not moving up in the congregational hierarchy at the same speed as men," she says. Only about a dozen women serve as senior rabbis in large congregations.

A Major Impact

Yet women are having an impact on "conversations about prayer and spirituality, interpretations of text, and recovering of history," she adds. For instance, the project to produce the soon-to-be published revision of the Reform prayer book was headed by a woman.

In Christianity, women's ordination has a long history. American women have pioneered new churches, including Mary Baker Eddy, who founded the Christian Science church, which publishes this newspaper; evangelist Aimee Semple McPherson, the Foursquare Church; and Ellen White, the Seventh-Day Adventist Church.

Still, the continuing debate (among Protestants) over New Testament language about women and the fact that Jesus' disciples were men (for Catholics) shores up the resistance to women leaders.

As Anglicans in the Church of England continue to address the question of women bishops, for example, one Oxford clergyman has written on the distinction between having women priests and bishops. Referring to Genesis, he writes: "God made man in his own image; in the image of God created he male and female . . . God's order is that the man is first in order and the woman second (equal in dignity but not in order)."

Ms. Rankin, with 23 years' experience as a pastor and district superintendent in the United Methodist Church, has encountered similar views. In a career that's been "an amazing ride," she has particularly loved preaching and helping nurture disciples. Yet she ponders whether there is a backlash under way.

In her most recent post as senior pastor of a 2,200-member church, she was surprised to "run into walls" over her role with some young congregants. "To see that among a conservative element of a new generation is disheartening," says the mother whose family has been very supportive over the years.

The ministry "is the hardest thing in the world to do and the most rewarding," she adds. "There's been pain and hurtful things, but also glorious moments. I can't imagine doing anything else."

Pioneers Serve as Mentors

Younger pastors have benefited from the work of such pioneers. Reverend Kershner attended Columbia Seminary in Decatur, Ga., where 50 percent of students were women. "I was affirmed in ways that were empowering," she says. After her 1999 ordination, she found an associate pastor post and became a senior pastor before she was 30. That remarkable event occurred in the conservative Texas Bible belt, no less, and after she attended the interview with her newborn baby. Yet she and the Presbyterian congregation of about 325 families seemed to agree her leadership role was what God had in mind.

"No one left as a result of me coming, and actually some folks came because it was something different," Kershner says.

The job has been challenging for a young mother of two (though her husband is a willing stay-at-home dad), who didn't expect the inherent loneliness or the constant emotional weight. "I carry these people around with me all the time, in my head and in my heart," she says. Still, she adds, "I consider it a privilege."

Kershner even takes a bit of mischievous delight in wearing her collar to ecumenical gatherings with conservative Baptists, where it always sparks discussion.

"There are some people concerned with the state of our souls," she says, "but we are OK with that."

> *"The ordination of women is not simply a matter of making a woman a priest. It is much more; it is the ultimate destruction of the Christian faith."*

The Ordination of Women Is a Negative Development in Religious Communities

Father John Morris

According to this viewpoint, the growing acceptance of women's ordination in various Christian denominations is an alarming development that threatens the foundations of traditional Christianity. The author contends that "feminist ideology" is responsible for women's ordination, which in turn has triggered a devaluing of biblical scripture and hallowed religious traditions and principles. The author of this viewpoint is Father John Morris, who serves as pastor of Forty Holy Martyrs of Sebaste Orthodox Mission in Stafford, Texas.

As you read, consider the following questions:

1. According to the author, how do feminists distort the priesthood and other positions of religious leadership?

Father John Morris, "Thoughts on Women's Ordination," *Word Magazine*, January 2004. Reproduced by permission of the author.

2. What church leadership positions does the author believe are acceptable for women?

3. In what ways does the author compare the feminist cause to a political campaign?

During the last part of the twentieth century, Feminism swept through society like a raging forest fire and has become one of the most significant developments in modern history. It is not an exaggeration to state that feminism has redefined almost every aspect of contemporary American culture.

Feminists and their supporters have demanded and received changes in the English language, which, like [author George] Orwell's "Newspeak," more correctly express the prejudices of their movement. Thus, it is no longer acceptable to say "mankind." Instead one must say "humankind." A postman is now a letter carrier. A fireman is now a firefighter and even clergymen are now clergypersons. In schools, young girls learn to be assertive and to reject traditional feminine qualities while boys are urged to "get in touch with their feminine side." In every place where radical feminists have gained a footing, their ideas have overwhelmed traditional beliefs in many different ways including religion. Not only have feminists demanded and received admission of women to the ordained ministry, they have also successfully persuaded many Christians to redefine their understanding of God to conform to the feminist ideology. . . .

If it is necessary to redefine God to conform to a secular ideology such as feminism, it is necessary to redefine everything else, thereby inventing a new, politically correct, feminized religion that only has a superficial similarity to traditional Christianity. In almost every case, one of the first steps in the feminization of religion is the ordination of women. During the last few decades virtually every Christian group, with the exception of a few more conservative Protestant bodies, the Roman Catholic Church and, of course, the Orthodox Church, has yielded to pressure from feminists and has admitted women to the ordained ministry. Significantly, the secular media has fallen into line with feminist ideology and speaks with derision about those Christian groups which still adhere to the ancient prohibition against the ordination of women. However, it is important to understand that the ordination of women is only part of a process that eventually leads to a rejection of Biblical and Traditional Christianity in favor of a new feminized and ultimately heretical religion. . . .

Historical Gender Roles

Although it may not satisfy those who seek a rational explanation, the historical practice of the Church may very well be the best argument against the ordination of women. One might ask, if it is wrong to deny women ordination, why would the Church, which is led by the Holy Spirit to manifest the will of God in society, be guilty of oppression against women by denying them their rightful place in the ranks of the clergy? Christ chose no women Apostles. The Church has never allowed women to become priests or bishops. Indeed, those few "Christian" groups in antiquity that allowed some form of women's ordination were far outside the mainstream of Christianity and were associated with Gnosticism and/or some other major heresy. That should be enough to convince any faithful Orthodox Christian that it would be the height of arrogance for some in the twenty-first century to claim they are qualified to declare that the Church has been wrong for almost 2,000 years.

Indeed, if it is an injustice to deny women ordination, why did not Christ Himself set the example by choosing women Apostles? Neither Christ nor his followers had the slightest inhibition against speaking out against the injustices of their time. If the denial of ordination were an injustice, one would expect that Christ, who criticized so many of the practices of the religious establishment of His day, would have set the example for his followers by naming at least one woman Apostle. . . .

Thus those who approach the priesthood must approach it on God's and His Church's terms, not their own terms or those of a secular ideology such as Feminism. The feminists also distort the priesthood, by turning what should be a ministry of service and self-sacrifice into a position of power and prestige. A priest is a servant, not a master. Indeed, if a man treats his priesthood as a position of power and authority, he has perverted his calling and yielded to the temptation to the greatest sin of all, the sin of pride. Indeed, if the priesthood were a position of power, it would be an injustice to deny it to women. However, the priesthood is only one of many ministries and leadership positions within the Church. Here the words of St. Paul are relevant:

> For by one Spirit we were all baptized into one body—Jews or Greeks, slaves or free—and all were made to drink of one Spirit. For the body does not consist of one member but of many. If the foot should say, "Because I am not a hand, I do not belong to the body," that would not make it any less a part of the body. And if the ear should say, "Because I am not an eye, I do not belong to the body," that would not make it any less a part of the body. If the whole body were an eye, where would be the hearing? If the whole body were an ear, where would be the sense of smell? But as it is, God arranged the organs in the body, each one of them, as he chose. If all were a single organ, where would the body be? As it is, there are many parts, yet one body. . . .

Female Leadership Positions

Despite the male priesthood, women occupy leadership positions within the Church. Women serve on parish councils, attend the conventions of their Archdiocese, and even serve on the Board of Trustees of their Archdiocese. They also are ministers of the Church because the ordained priesthood is but one of many ministries in the Church. The woman who directs a choir or teaches Sunday School is just as much a minister as a priest or bishop. A priest must first of all be humble before God and before those whom he is called to serve. A radical feminist demanding ordination as a "right," is anything but humble and therefore fails to meet one of the most important requirements of the priesthood.

Radical feminism distorts not only the priesthood but also the very nature of humanity by failing to recognize that there are real differences between men and women. A man cannot be a mother, nor a mother a father. By attempting to blur the distinction between the genders, the feminists are distorting the very essence of human nature. They also fail to understand that the roles of the different sexes are complementary and follow the plan of creation designed by God. To act as if men and women are the same in every way is to deny one of the most basic facts of human existence. Because men and women are different, God has decreed as we know through the practice of the Church that men and women should have different, but complementary roles in the Church. That women and men are different and occupy different positions within the Church does not mean that one is superior to the other. This is one of the most basic flaws of the radical feminist argument. They fail to recognize that equality does not require sameness. Men and women can play different roles in the leadership of the Church and still remain equal to one another in every way.

However, perhaps the most important argument against the ordination of women is the results of women's ordination in those Christian groups who have surrendered to the pressure of secular society to ordain women. A priest is not simply a performer or leader; a priest is an image of Christ who in turn is an image of God. Thus, a priest is an icon or symbol of Christ, especially during the Divine Liturgy. Because symbols have real meaning, if the symbol is changed, that

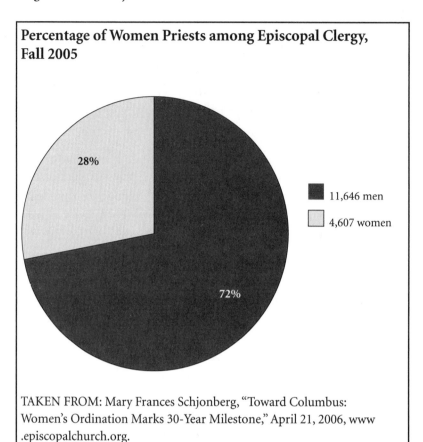

Percentage of Women Priests among Episcopal Clergy, Fall 2005

28%

72%

■ 11,646 men

□ 4,607 women

TAKEN FROM: Mary Frances Schjonberg, "Toward Columbus: Women's Ordination Marks 30-Year Milestone," April 21, 2006, www .episcopalchurch.org.

which is symbolized is also changed. Since a priest represents Christ, who is God, if the priest becomes a priestess, the image of God also changes. This will inevitably lead to a redefinition, or to use their term, "re-imaging" of God. . . .

The Dangers of Feminist Theology

Virtually every Protestant group that has decided to ordain women has to one degree or another begun to reject Biblical language and images of God in favor of images more acceptable to feminist theology.

Thus, God is no longer Father, Son and Holy Spirit, but becomes "Creator, Redeemer, and Sanctifier." On the surface this may seem only a change of terms, but actually, it is much more. It represents a radically different way of looking at God. The new politically correct Trinity is a rejection of divinely revealed language about God and thereby a rejection of the divine inspiration of the Holy Scriptures. It is also heretical because it blurs the important distinction between the Father, Son and Holy Spirit. The Father also creates, redeems and sanctifies, but so does the Son and the Holy Spirit. In reality, the feminized Trinity is actually a form of the ancient heresy of Sabellianism, which portrays Father, Son and Holy Spirit as merely different phases of God rather than different but united persons.

Not only have the feminists redefined God to accommodate their ideology, they have begun to redefine the entire Christian religion in the light of feminism. Thus, they place their secular ideology above the divine revelation of God in the Holy Scriptures and the other manifestations of Holy Tradition. This is the ultimate secularization of the Gospel, because they have subordinated the divinely inspired Scriptures and other manifestations of Holy Tradition to a secular ideology.

Indeed, anyone who has watched the efforts of followers of feminism and its allied ideologies to redefine American Protestantism sees not prayerful contemplation in an effort to discern the will of God, but the very worst aspects of an organized political campaign by one group to gain power over another. Thus, feminists eventually beat down their opponents because they are more persistent and effective political organizers than the opponents.

A Heretical Movement

Borrowing methods from the Civil Rights Movement, these campaigns include rallies, demonstrations, intimidation and civil disobedience. Eventually, although originally a minority, they are able to prevail because the leadership of most American Protestant groups lacks the courage to dismiss or remove anyone who rejects traditional beliefs and practices. Indeed, today it is unacceptable to accuse someone of heresy, much less discipline them or remove them from their office in the Church. This attitude has led to a complete breakdown of anything like traditional Christianity among many American Protestants and even some Roman Catholics.

Thus, the ordination of women is not simply a matter of making a woman a priest. It is much more; it is the ultimate destruction of the Christian Faith. This is because the ordination of women requires the rejection of the clear practice of the Church and thereby of the Holy Scriptures and other manifestations of Holy Tradition. It is also because the movement to ordain women does not come from within the Christian community, but is actually the subordination of the Faith to the secular ideology of Feminism. Once one rationalizes the rejection of something as central to the Faith as the nature of the priesthood, it then becomes easier to reject anything else in the Tradition of the Church that followers of that ideology find offensive. If one takes it upon oneself to decide which beliefs and practices of the Church are acceptable to modern society, the result is the chaos that has engulfed American Protestantism and has even made its influence felt in Roman Catholic circles.

Thus, if one decides that the Church has been wrong to deny the priesthood to women, one might also decide that the Church has been wrong in other beliefs and practices. Indeed, this is precisely what has happened. Despite centuries of opposition to abortion by Christians, almost every major American Protestant group that has ordained women has also adopted a "pro-choice" position on abortion. Recently, the Episcopal Church elected as a bishop a man who left his wife and children to live in a homosexual relationship with another man. There can be no doubt that not only the Holy Scriptures, but also the Fathers and the Ecumenical Councils consider homosexual acts immoral. Indeed, there is also no doubt that until a very few years ago, every Christian group, Protestant, Orthodox, or Roman Catholic, taught that homosexual sexual acts are a fundamental violation of the moral law of God.

A Slippery Slope

However, it is also true that until fairly recently, all Christian groups agreed that only men could be ordained. If Christians can decide that the unanimous opinion of Christians throughout the centuries is wrong on one issue, the ordination of women, it is logical to assume that Christians can also be wrong on other issues such as abortion and homosexuality, especially since the same feminists who demand women's ordination are also frequently sympathetic to so-called gay liberation. Thus, because they see everything in the light of feminism, they no longer accept Traditional images of God. They redefine the Holy Trinity in completely unbiblical language because of the dictates of their ideology.

They also redefine Christian morality to conform to the demands of radical feminism, which has a strong affinity to the gay liberation movement. This eventually leads to a complete perversion of the Gospel. The gospel of feminism and political correctness no longer calls humans to repentance and righteous living, but demands the acceptance of the right to each person to be free to live according to his or her own standards, even if those standards clearly conflict with the standards of Holy Scripture. Indeed, according to this criterion, any demand that one seek any other personal value than self-fulfillment according to one's own needs, is bigoted and to be rejected in favor of inclusiveness.

That is one major reason why every American Protestant group that has begun to ordain women has also begun to feel pressure from many of the same people who successfully campaigned for women's ordination to recognize homosexual and lesbian relationships as equal to heterosexual marriage. Thus, the ordination of women to the priesthood is not simply the acceptance of women priests. It leads to a complete distortion of the Christian Faith and the creation of a new religion that has only a very superficial resemblance to any form of traditional Christianity.

"I have come to realize that I am effective in ministry not despite the fact that I am homosexual, but often because I am homosexual."

Homosexuals Belong in Positions of Religious Leadership

Anonymous

In this viewpoint, a homosexual Catholic priest who has maintained his vow of celibacy laments the refusal of Church leaders to accept openly homosexual priests. He argues that this hostility to homosexual clergy is un-Christian and that it will ultimately have a negative impact on countless Catholic communities. The author of this viewpoint is a Catholic priest who requested anonymity out of concern for potential professional consequences. His request was granted by Commonweal, *the publisher of the viewpoint.*

As you read, consider the following questions:

1. What does the author say is his own mother's attitude toward homosexuals?

Anonymous, "Made in God's Image: A Homosexual Priest Speaks Out," *Commonweal*, vol. 130, April 11, 2003. Copyright © 2003 Commonweal Publishing Co., Inc. Reproduced by permission of Commonweal Foundation.

2. How does the author believe that his homosexual sexual orientation has helped him be a better priest?

3. According to the author, what will be the ultimate result of an outright ban on the ordination of homosexual men, even if they are celibate?

I understand the struggle homosexual people have believing that they are made in God's image, that they are good, that official church teaching can serve as the foundation for a healthy, grace-filled spirituality. I am saddened that it is the authorities of the church I love who have placed the biggest obstacle to acceptance of such goodness, asking that we see ourselves as "disoriented" toward a corrupt end.

I knew that I was called to priesthood before I knew that I was gay. The lure of sacramental mystery that resonated with my young soul, the ready acceptance I found in my home parish community, and the care and attention shown me by priests of all ages and temperaments convinced me at an early age that my life would be spent in service as a priest. The excitement, complexity, and beauty of my sexuality were a later discovery, coming at a time when body, mind, and soul were ready to explore and understand one of God's most profound gifts. Yes, I knew that I was called to priesthood before I knew that I was gay. That is why the recent pronouncements from Rome and elsewhere that homosexuals are not fit for priesthood give me pause and cause me to wonder, "How could that be?"

Though disheartened and angered by the growing number of voices judging me unfit, I am not surprised. It has been my experience that even the most loving people fall prey to intolerance when it comes to the topic of homosexuality. Once when I tried to talk with my mother about my ministry to gay and lesbian students at a local college, her only response was, "I hate those people." And during a time of personal challenge when I "came out" to a pastor I loved like a father, he told me, "Funny, you don't look like one of them."

The Mission Remains the Same

There is not a shred of evidence that lesbians and gay men—whether "out" or not—are any less able or willing to love God and neighbor than heterosexuals; no evidence of their being less adept at feeding the hungry, welcoming the stranger, or visiting the sick; no evidence of less commitment to the weighty matters of justice, mercy, and faith. In relation to ordination, there is no evidence that lesbians and gay men are less capable in service, word, sacrament, and order, nor in conviction and confidence in God's call to ordained ministry.

William M. McElvaney, "Why Should the Church Allow Ordination of Gay Men and Lesbians?" In Finishing the Journey: Questions and Answers from United Methodists of Conviction. *Dallas, TX: Northaven United Methodist Church, 2006.*

No, I am not surprised. I think I have been expecting this to happen for some time. Still, hearing the words that pronounce me unsuitable hurt and confuse me. If Rome decides that homosexuals will not be admitted to the priesthood, then I will be an unwelcome member of a brotherhood whose defining character is the attraction to women. How did I get here? How is it that I now find myself feeling like the guest who entered the wedding feast not properly clothed? Why wasn't I stopped at the door before ordination twenty-five years ago?

Struggles in Seminary

Throughout my seven years of seminary formation, I struggled with the issue of my same-sex attraction and wondered whether it was possible for me to respond to the call to priesthood, given the church's teaching and understanding of the issue. The call to ministry was clear to me and apparently to many others, including family, friends, priests I had known, and seminary personnel. Still, the question remained: Could I live a happy, meaningful celibate life in service to others, knowing that the church I wanted to serve considered an integral part of my person to be "basically disordered"?

As questions emerged each step of the way there was always a spiritual director to guide me, and, for a two-year period, a priest counselor who challenged me to understand the role my sexuality played in my self-appreciation and how I related to others. In the prayer life of the seminary, in the direction I received from spiritual guides and confessors, and in the supportive community of my brother seminarians, I found the strength and acceptance I needed to continue toward ordination.

It puzzles me that those who now oppose the ordination of homosexuals argue that living in a seminary environment might make it more difficult to live chastely (see Andrew R. Baker, "Ordination and Same-Sex Attraction," *America*, September 30, 2002). Every article and book I have read encourages those who want to live in accord with the church's teaching on homosexuality to develop a strong life of prayer, to seek a supportive spiritual director, and to be part of a community that shares the church's teaching. Far from being a source of temptation, the seminary ought to be the optimal place where one can find direction and support in living a chaste life. The assumption that an all-male seminary would be an occasion of temptation for gay men is absurd. Does that mean that hearing confessions in a convent would be an occasion of temptation for a heterosexual priest and thus should be avoided? Of course not. Why is it that sexuality is always reduced to sexual urges rather than being understood in the larger context of how one relates as a whole person—body, mind, and spirit?

A Loving Relationship with God

I also find it disturbing that issues sometimes associated with homosexuals (Baker suggests substance abuse, sexual addiction, and depression) are thought of as intrinsically related to homosexuality, rather than resulting from a poorly formed sexual identity. It would stand to reason: if a homosexual man starts with the assumption that his sexuality is disordered because, as Baker says, it "tends toward a corrupt end" and can "never image God and never contribute to the good of the person or society," he might have to struggle with feelings of maladjustment or depression. Those unhealthy attitudes and potentially self-destructive behaviors stem not from the orientation itself but from the destructive self-image imposed on homosexuals by society and the church. If I were to believe that the God-given gift of my sexuality is disordered, how would I ever establish a trusting, loving relationship with the God who so ordered me? Living a celibate life does not erase one's sexuality. It challenges the celibate to direct all relational energy (heterosexual or homosexual) in loving service to those to whom we minister. That relational energy is more than genital expression; it is the whole self in relation to others. It is a puzzle to me that writers like Baker who voice such strong opinions on this subject reduce sexuality to physical attraction.

The twenty-five years I have spent in priestly ministry have been years of challenge, grace, and a sharing in the mystery of the incarnate God made visible in Jesus, who continues to live in and through his church. The person of the priest is called to mirror the selfless, chaste love of Christ to those he serves. He does so not because he is heterosexual; he does so because he is willing to reaffirm the goodness of people made in God's image and likeness, calling them to live the gospel message in the face of misunderstanding, challenge, and sacrifice. I have come to realize that I am effective in ministry, not despite the fact that I am homosexual, but often because I am homosexual.

I know it is difficult for some to understand that assertion. That may be because writers like George Weigel (*The Courage to Be Catholic*) divide homosexual people into two types: gays ("a man who makes his homoerotic desires the center of his personality and identity") and those who recognize their homosexual desires to be disordered. Such an analysis reduces the choices a homosexual person makes to either promiscuity or self-abnegation. Neither choice leads to a healthy spirituality based on an appreciation of being made in God's image and likeness. Another option is needed, one that defines the multifaceted dimensions of sexuality and reflects the limitless love God has for his beloved. There is no such thing as generic divine love: God's love is always directed in unique, jealous fashion to each person as beloved. So too is the unique response of the individual to God's grace, which builds on one's nature, be it heterosexual or homosexual.

Made in God's Image

Because official church teaching denies such a possibility for homosexuals, I understand the struggle homosexual people have believing that they are made in God's image, that they are good, that official church teaching can serve as the foundation for a healthy, grace-filled spirituality. I am saddened that it is the authorities of the church I love who have placed the biggest obstacle to acceptance of such goodness, asking that we see ourselves as "disoriented" toward a corrupt end. It is one of the heavy burdens, hard to carry, that the church places on many of her sons and daughters. Woe to those who impose such a burden!

It will be a sad day for me if those in authority decide to impose a ban on the ordination of homosexual men, and it will be a sad day for the whole church. Many of us will be lost, for I suspect there will be those who, out of self-respect and a decision not to accept the church's faulty designation, will choose to walk quietly out of the ministry to which God has called them, the ministry that they love. I suspect those in high places will hardly notice or will breathe a sigh of relief.

Those who have trusted and treasured their ministry, however, will notice and be saddened that their own spiritual welfare is being compromised once again by those who have the authority from Christ to make decisions, but lack his mind and heart to make them wisely.

> *"Someone afflicted with S.S.A. [same sex attraction] cannot redirect his inclination toward a complementary 'other' in a spousal relationship, because homosexuality has disordered his sexual attraction toward the opposite sex. It then becomes difficult to be genuinely a sign of Christ's spousal love for the church."*

Homosexuals Do Not Belong in Positions of Religious Leadership

Andrew R. Baker

According to this viewpoint, men and women who harbor "same sex attraction" or "S.S.A." are unsuitable for priesthood in the Catholic Church. The author asserts that people with S.S.A. are more likely to have "personal defects" that can hinder their ability to carry out priestly duties and that their homosexual desires make it impossible for them to partake of the "spousal union" between Christ and the Church. Reverend Andrew R. Baker is a

Andrew R. Baker, "Ordination and Same Sex Attraction," *America*, vol. 187, September 30, 2002. Copyright 2002 www.americamagazine.org. All rights reserved. Reproduced by permission of America Press. For subscription information, visit www.americamagazine.org.

priest of the Diocese of Allentown, Pennsylvania, and a member of the staff of the Congregation for Bishops in Rome.

As you read, consider the following questions:

1. How does the author define homosexuality within the context of suitability for ordination?
2. Does the author view same-sex attraction, in and of itself, as a sin?
3. In what ways does the author see homosexual cliques in seminaries as a serious problem?

Every bishop possesses the sacred duty of discerning the suitability of candidates for holy orders. St. Paul's advice to Timothy is fitting for all bishops, especially today [2002]: "Do not lay hands too readily on anyone" (1 Tim. 5: 22). The church's life and the way it manifests itself as the sacrament of salvation for the entire world leans inextricably on the shoulders of her priests. The supernatural "health," one could say, of the church depends heavily on the fitness of candidates for ordination.

In the aftermath of the scandal of clerical sexual abuse of minors, the church and society have focused partly on the role of homosexuality. The question has arisen as to whether or not it is advisable for a bishop to admit a man with predominantly homosexual tendencies, or what some call "same sex attraction" (S.S.A.), to the seminary and/or present him for holy orders.

Judging Suitability for Ordination

Thanks to a recent *Circular Letter* in 1997 from the Congregation for Divine Worship and the Discipline of the Sacraments concerning the suitability of candidates for holy orders, some guidance and assistance from the Holy See have already been given in order to tackle the thorny and difficult issue of suitability.

The letter says that a vocation is based on "a moral certitude that is founded upon positive reasons regarding the *suitability* of the candidate." Next, it mentions the fundamental reason not to admit a candidate to holy orders. The document says: "Admission may not take place if there exists a prudent doubt regarding the candidate's suitability. By 'prudent doubt' is meant a doubt founded upon facts that are objective and duly verified." Later, the congregation advises that it would seem "more appropriate to dismiss a doubtful candidate" than to lament the sadness and scandal of a cleric abandoning the ministry.

In other words, the congregation seems to suggest that even if there is only a "prudent doubt," based on objective facts, about the suitability of any candidate, the best and safest course of action is not to admit him to holy orders. The church does not ask for certitude that a man does not have a vocation but simply that a doubt has arisen through a prudent examination of evidence. Even though there may be a *lack of certitude* but a *definite prudent doubt*, a proper ecclesiastical authority should judge the candidate to be unsuitable.

What about a candidate with S.S.A.? Does it introduce a prudent doubt about suitability resulting in not admitting an applicant to a formation program or not issuing the call to holy orders?

The Meaning of Homosexuality

In order to determine the existence of a "prudent doubt," it would be helpful to clarify the meaning of the term "homosexuality." The *Catechism of the Catholic Church* describes it as "an exclusive or predominant sexual attraction toward persons of the same sex." Some may experience a wide range of intensity or different types of attractions to persons of the same sex, as some experts propose. Although, in the context of determining suitability for ordination, it would seem appropriate to limit the definition of the term "homosexuality" to describe

The Vatican Comments on "Homosexual Tendencies"

Concerning profoundly deep-rooted homosexual tendencies, that one discovers in a certain number of men and women, these are also objectively disordered and often constitute a trial, even for these men and women. These people must be received with respect and delicacy; one will avoid every mark of unjust discrimination with respect to them. These are called to realize the will of God in their lives and to unite to the Sacrifice of the Lord the difficulties that they may encounter.

In light of this teaching, this department, in agreement with the Congregation for Divine Worship and the Discipline of the Sacraments, holds it necessary clearly to affirm that the Church, while profoundly respecting the persons in question, may not admit to the seminary and Holy Orders those who practice homosexuality, show profoundly deep-rooted homosexual tendencies, or support the so-called gay culture.

The above persons find themselves, in fact, in a situation that gravely obstructs a right way of relating with men and women. The negative consequences that may derive from the Ordination of persons with profoundly deep-rooted homosexual tendencies are by no means to be ignored.

Catholic World News, translation of Vatican document on homosexuality and seminaries by Congregation for Catholic Education, November 4, 2005, www.cwnews.com.

those with *exclusive* or *predominant* tendencies, because a "prudent doubt" can be better verified objectively based on the clear presence of the disorder. With this clear information, a bishop can then make his decision concerning suitability.

Some have described S.S.A. as a sexual "orientation." At first glance, this description may seem to have some merit. The sexual attraction of someone with S.S.A. is "toward" persons of the same sex, and this "tending toward" could easily be described as an "orientation." However, to classify homosexuality as an "orientation" may obfuscate the serious *disorder* that exists and the distortion that has been introduced into a biblically inspired Christian anthropology.

Genesis speaks of God creating an image of himself by making man "male and female." In this dual and complementary relationship of persons, man finds within himself or can, in a certain sense, "read" in his body and in the body of a person of the opposite sex, a tendency to "leave his father and mother" and "cling" to the other (Gen. 2:24). The sexual orientation, the "tending toward" another of the opposite sex, is "written" in man's created constitution. It is part of what Pope John Paul II calls the "nuptial meaning of the body." Any other tendency to "cling" to another (be it to persons of the same sex, children, beasts, objects) is an aberration of the divine economy in which God reveals himself by creating an image of himself in the orientation of male to female and female to male.

The "Disorientation" of Same-Sex Attraction

The "orientation" of those who have another attraction, other than the divinely constituted one, is not a true "orientation." It would be better described as a *"disorientation."* It is fundamentally flawed in its disordered attraction because it can never "image" God and never contribute to the good of the person or society. This is why the Catholic Church teaches that the disorientation of homosexuality is "objectively disordered." Homosexuality may be an inclination, tendency or condition but it is fundamentally "dis-orienting" in that it tends toward a corrupt end. The attraction as such is *not* a sin. Only when one chooses to pursue the attraction in thought or deed does the disordered inclination become a disordered, and therefore sinful, choice.

Nevertheless, homosexual tendencies are aberrations that can and should be addressed by both the individual and by competent experts with the aid of behavioral sciences as well as by spiritual means, including prayer, the sacraments and spiritual direction. According to some experts, S.S.A. can be treated and even prevented with some degree of success. But does it introduce a "prudent doubt" when determining suitability for ordination?

There are a number of significant negative aspects to S.S.A. that contribute to a "prudent doubt" with regard to the suitability of a candidate for holy orders.

First and foremost among them is the possible simultaneous manifestation of other serious problems such as substance abuse, sexual addiction and depression. With more than one serious disorder, a candidate may find it difficult to respond to the demands of formation, and the seminary or religious house may struggle to accommodate the extra needs involved in the healing process of the individual.

Likewise, there is an increased possibility that persons with S.S.A. may be more familiar with certain patterns and techniques of deception and repression, either conscious or subconscious, which were learned in trying to deal with their tendencies in a largely heterosexual environment. After years of hiding or of being confused about their abnormal attractions, it is possible that duplicitous or pretentious behaviors could appear. These kinds of personal defects make the moral formation of the candidate much more difficult and can negatively affect the formation of the other candidates.

Other Problems with Gay Priesthood

Another aspect that would contribute to a "prudent doubt" concerning a candidate with S.S.A. is a question about his adherence to church teaching. There are many men and women with S.S.A. who uphold and defend the church's teaching on homosexuality. But if someone with S.S.A. is insecure about dealing straightforwardly with his disordered attractions or has some doubts about their disordered character, he may tend to possess a distorted and erroneous view of human sexuality. Thus, there exists the risk that such an individual will struggle with or even deny the clear teaching of the church regarding his disordered inclinations and any acts that might flow from these tendencies.

Part of the distortion of S.S.A. is the tendency to view the other person of the same sex as a possible sexual "partner" or even to reduce the other (also a temptation for heterosexuals) to a sexual object. In such a clearly male environment as the seminary and the priesthood, the temptation is ever-present for those with the disorder. This temptation could present very difficult circumstances and the overwhelming presentation of the object of their attraction (men), which is naturally part of an all-male and intensely close community, could make their efforts to live chastely or to be healed of their disorder very difficult.

Furthermore, as has been the unfortunate experience in some seminaries and dioceses, cliques may form based on the disordered attractions. This could hamper the healing process that might be possible for some, because the effeminate affective manners and a certain "acceptability" of the disorder are often promoted in such groups. Also these cliques can confuse young heterosexual men in the growth of their understanding of manhood and in developing skills and virtues to live a celibate life, because they can often see modeled in members of these cliques a disordered view of human sexuality and of proper masculine behavior.

The Question of Celibacy

Another question for determining suitability for a candidate with S.S.A. is whether the individual can live celibacy. Celibacy is a vocational choice to which one is bound by a vow or promise to live chastely for the sake of the kingdom of God by foregoing the good of marriage and family life. It is a sign of one's identification with Christ, one's availability for service to the church and of the spousal union between Christ and the church in the kingdom of God.

People with homosexual tendencies can live certain aspects of celibacy, but their commitment is significantly different from that of heterosexuals because it compromises two fundamental dimensions of celibacy.

On the one hand, celibacy involves a sacrifice of a good for a greater good. It sacrifices ordered and good inclinations toward spouse and family for the sake of the kingdom. For someone with S.S.A., an act of binding oneself by a vow or promise to abstain from something that one is already bound to avoid by the natural law (attractions toward someone of the same sex) seems superfluous. To avoid doing something (heterosexual acts) that one does not have an inclination to do is not a sacrifice. The struggle to live chastely may be extremely difficult for someone with homosexual tendencies, and these struggles would truly be meritorious and virtuous as acts of *chastity*, but not necessarily of celibacy.

Likewise, the spousal dimension of celibacy seems unclear for those with S.S.A. Celibacy is a way of living the spousal character of Christ's relationship with his bride, the church. Through the celibate life, the priest redirects his sexual attraction to the opposite sex toward another "body," the church, which is a "bride" in a complementary spousal relationship. He exercises a spiritual fatherhood and lives a supernatural spousal relationship as a sign to the church of Christ's love for her. Someone afflicted with S.S.A. cannot redirect his inclination toward a complementary "other" in a spousal relationship, because homosexuality has disordered his sexual attraction toward the opposite sex. It then becomes difficult to be genuinely a sign of Christ's spousal love for the church.

Celibacy Is Not Enough

If it can be said that a man with homosexual tendencies can live a celibate life, at the very least it is lacking some important elements due to S.S.A., and it could be another reason to conclude that there exists a prudent doubt as to his suitability for holy orders.

It would seem that if there are firmly established facts, both from an objective psychological evaluation and an examination in the external forum of past and present behavior and choices, that a man does indeed suffer from S.S.A. as an "exclusive or predominant sexual attraction toward persons of the same sex" (*Catechism*, No. 2357), then he should not be admitted to holy orders, and his presence in the seminary would not only give him false hope but it may, in fact, hinder the needed therapy and healing that might come from appropriate psychological and spiritual care. It may be that a man could be healed of such a disorder and then he could be considered for admission to the seminary and possibly to Holy Orders, but not while being afflicted with the disorder.

The Pauline exhortation not to "lay hands too readily on anyone" is a heavy responsibility for any bishop; but if a candidate's suitability is scrutinized with prudence, the act of "laying on of hands" will bear abundant fruit in the lives of those who will be touched by the ministry of a priest.

Periodical Bibliography

The following articles have been selected to supplement the diverse views presented in this chapter.

Jennifer Ferrera and Sarah Hinlicky Wilson	"Ordaining Women: Two Views," *First Things*, April 2003.
John Garvey	"Priests Should Be Married," *Commonweal*, August 12, 2005.
Danielle Harder	"Keeping the Faith," *Herizons*, Spring 2004.
Todd Henneman	"Scared of Sex," *Advocate*, August 17, 2004.
John C. LaRue Jr.	"Pastors, Marriage, and Sexual Temptation," *Your Church*, March–April 2005.
Joe Maxwell	"Devastated by an Affair," *Christianity Today*, January 2007.
Lisa Miller	"Life in Solitary," *Newsweek*, June 20, 2005.
Randall R. Phillips	"Gift or Curse?" *Commonweal*, September 10, 2004.
Anna Quindlen	"Complex and Contradictory," *Newsweek*, April 18, 2005.
Andrew Sullivan	"The Vatican's New Stereotype: Why Its New Rules Barring Gay Priests Turn Jesus' Teaching on Its Head," *Time*, December 12, 2005.
Gerard Thomas [pseud.]	"A Gay Priest Speaks Out," *Commonweal*, January 28, 2005.
Mira Tweti	"Daughters of the Buddha," *Tricycle*, Winter 2006.
Edward Vacek	"Acting More Humanely: Accepting Gays into the Priesthood," *America*, December 16, 2002.
N.T. Wright	"The Biblical Basis for Women's Service in the Church," *Priscilla Papers*, Autumn 2006.

For Further Discussion

Chapter 1

1. Don Lattin and Roger Scruton have starkly different views about whether the so-called "Sexual Revolution" of the 1960s has been good or bad for American morality and attitudes about sexuality. Whose argument do you find more convincing, and why?

2. Pamela Toussaint's essay explains the religious foundations of Lakita Garth's decision to remain abstinent until marriage. Garth's basic philosophy is supported by Lauren F. Winner's essay, but Rabbi Balfour Brickner argues that sexual activity in a loving relationship—even if not a formal marriage—is not sinful. Which viewpoint do you find to be stronger? Explain your reasoning.

Chapter 2

1. The first two essays in this chapter use scriptural passages from the Bible to support their perspective on homosexuality—yet one of the essays condemns homosexuality on moral grounds while the other defends gay sexuality and gay rights. Which arguments carry more weight with you? Why? Which arguments seem misleading or otherwise intellectually dishonest? Explain the reasons behind your view.

2. Dan Savage's essay asserts that opposition to gay marriage is based primarily on homophobia. The Vatican, however, cites scriptural passages in declaring its opposition to same-sex marriage. With these positions in mind, do you think Savage's accusation has merit? Why or why not?

3. Civil unions have been discussed as a possible "compromise" position in the battle between those who support same-sex marriage and those who oppose it. Jim Wallis makes the case for civil unions, but Peter Wood argues against the concept. Wood's opposition, though, stems from his belief that any legal recognition of same-sex couples is morally wrong. What arguments, though, can you think of to oppose civil unions from a *liberal* position? That is, why might advocates of same-sex marriage oppose the idea of civil unions?

Chapter 3

1. In the abortion debate that exists in churches and communities across the United States, each side accuses the other of using dishonest rhetoric to advance its cause. As you read the essays in this chapter, identify two arguments used by each side (four in all) that you believe are misleading, deceptive, exaggerated, or otherwise unfair or untrue. Explain why you believe these arguments are flawed—and whether they detract from the strength of their other arguments. Then identify the two arguments used by each side that you think are strongest. Explain your selections.

2. Christine A. Scheller and the Religious Coalition for Reproductive Choice differ in their perspective on whether abortion should be defended or condemned by Christians and people of other faiths. In what ways do they agree? In what ways do they disagree?

Chapter 4

1. In their essays, Robert Barron and Alan Phillip reach totally different conclusions about whether the Catholic Church should abandon its rules of celibacy for its priests. Which perspective do you find most persuasive? Explain why. What do you think is the weakest argument presented by the opposing essay? Why?

2. The number of women clergy has grown enormously in the last part of the twentieth and first part of the twenty-first centuries in many parts of the country. What factors do you think might account for this increase?

3. The last two essays in this chapter debate whether gay people belong in positions of religious leadership. With which perspective do you most agree? Explain your choice.

Organizations to Contact

The editors have compiled the following list of organizations concerned with the issues debated in this book. The descriptions are derived from materials provided by the organizations. All have publications or information available for interested readers. The list was compiled on the date of publication of the present volume; the information provided here may change. Readers need to remember that many organizations take several weeks or longer to respond to inquiries.

Alan Guttmacher Institute
120 Wall St., New York, NY   10005
(212) 248-1111 • fax: (212) 248-1951
e-mail: info@guttmacher.org
Web site: www.guttmacher.org

The institute works to protect and expand the reproductive choices of all women and men. It strives to ensure that people have access to the information and services they need to exercise their rights and responsibilities concerning sexual activity, reproduction, and family planning. Among the institute's publications are *Abortion in Women's Lives, Adding It Up: The Benefits of Investing in Sexual and Reproductive Health Care,* and the periodical *Perspectives on Sexual and Reproductive Health.*

Catholics for a Free Choice
1436 U St. NW, Ste. 301, Washington, DC   20009-3997
(202) 986-6093 • fax: (202) 332-7995
e-mail: cffc@catholicsforchoice.org
Web site: www.catholicsforchoice.org

Catholics for a Free Choice is an advocacy group for Catholics who support a woman's moral and legal right to follow her conscience in matters of sexuality, reproductive freedom, and reproductive health. It conducts education and advocacy work in the United States, Europe, and Latin America. Publications produced by Catholics for a Free Choice include *Sex in the HIV/AIDS Era* and *You Are Not Alone: Information for Catholic Women on the Abortion Decision*. The organization also produces *Conscience*, a quarterly magazine.

Dignity USA
PO Box 15373, Washington, DC   20003
(202) 861-0017 • fax: (202) 543-5511
e-mail: info@dignityusa.org
Web site: www.dignityusa.org

Dignity USA is a Catholic organization of gay, lesbian, bisexual, and transgender persons who worship together and advocate for increased GLBT rights within the official church and in U.S. society. *Breath of the Spirit* is a weekly electronic newsletter made available to members and friends of Dignity USA.

Family Research Council
810 G St. NW, Washington, DC   20001
(202) 393-2100 • fax: (202) 393-2134
Web site: www.frc.org

The council is a research, resource, and education organization that promotes traditional marriage and traditional family structure as the foundations of a healthy and moral civilization. The organization also believes that government has a duty to promote and protect traditional marriage in law and public policy. The organization's publications include *Getting It Straight: What the Research Shows about Homosexuality; The Bible, the Church, and Homosexuality* and *Protecting Your Child in an X-Rated World*.

Focus on the Family
Colorado Springs, CO   80995
(719) 531-5181 • fax: (719) 531-3424
e-mail: info@family.org
Web site: www.family.org

Focus on the Family is a conservative Christian organization that promotes traditional marriage and Bible-based perspectives on moral issues as part of its larger mission of evangelism. It also actively campaigns against abortion, homosexuality, pornography, sexual activity outside of traditional marriage, divorce, and other perceived threats to Christian society. Organization publications include the *Focus on the Family Marriage Series: A Parents' Guide to Preventing Homosexuality, And the Bride Wore White*, and *Why You Can't Stay Silent: A Biblical Mandate to Shape Our Culture.*

Institute for Marriage and Public Policy (IMAPP)
PO Box 1231, Manassas, VA   20108
(202) 216-9430
e-mail: info@imapp.org
Web site: www.imapp.org

The Institute for Marriage and Public Policy is a nonprofit research and education organization that seeks to find ways in which law and public policy can strengthen traditional marriage as a social institution. Special areas of research and discussion include same-sex marriage, pregnancy outside of marriage, gender roles, and divorce law. IMAPP reports include *Do Mothers and Fathers Matter?* and *Marriage and the Law: A Statement of Principles.*

National Organization for Women (NOW)
1100 H St. NW, Third Floor, Washington, DC   20005
(202) 628-8669 • fax: (202) 785-8576
Web site: www.now.org

The National Organization for Women is the largest organization of feminist activists in the United States, with more than 500,000 contributing members. NOW is dedicated to bringing about social and economic equality for women, and a significant part of its advocacy work is concerned with securing abortion, birth control, and reproductive rights for all women. NOW publishes a quarterly magazine, *National NOW Times.*

National Sexuality Resource Center (NSRC)

2017 Mission St., Ste. 300, San Francisco, CA   94110
(415) 437-5121
e-mail: nsrcinfo@sfsu.edu
Web site: http://nsrcs.sfsu.edu

The NSRC is a project of the Human Sexuality Studies Program at San Francisco State University. The mission of the center is to advance sexual literacy through science, sexuality education, and social policy formation. It also works to counter what it views as negative and distorted representations of sexuality by conservative religious and social organizations and policymakers. Periodicals published by the National Sexuality Resource Center include *Sexual Literacy, American Sexuality*, and *Sexuality Research & Social Policy.*

Planned Parenthood Federation of America (PPFA)

434 West Thirty-Third St., New York, NY   10001
(212) 541-7800 • fax: (212) 245-1845
e-mail: member-services@ppfa.org
Web site: www.plannedparenthood.org

Planned Parenthood believes individuals have the right to make their own reproductive choices without interference from government or other individuals. It promotes comprehensive sex education and provides contraceptive counseling and services through more than 860 centers across the United States. Publications available through the organization include *How to Talk with Your Child About Sex, Human Sexuality: What Children Need to Know*, and *How Abortion Is Provided.*

Religious Coalition for Reproductive Choice (RCRC)

1025 Vermont Ave NW, Ste. 1130, Washington, DC   20005
(202) 628-7700 • fax: (202) 628-7716
e-mail: info@rcrc.org
Web site: www.rcrc.org

The Religious Coalition for Reproductive Choice is an alliance of religious organizations dedicated to using education and advocacy to preserve reproductive choice in the United States.

Special areas of emphasis in RCRC advocacy include representing poor people, people of color, and other "underserved" populations in debates about reproductive issues. Publications offered by the RCRC include *Between a Woman and Her God: Clergy and Women Tell Their Stories* and *Words of Choice: Countering Anti-Choice Rhetoric*.

Religious Institute on Sexual Morality, Justice, and Healing
304 Main Ave., Ste. 335, Norwalk, CT   06851
e-mail: info@religiousinstitute.org
Web site: www.religiousinstitute.org

The institute is an ecumenical, interfaith organization dedicated to advocating for sexual health, education, and justice in religious communities and U.S. society. It seeks to educate lawmakers, religious institutions, clergy, and laypersons about ways in which sex education can be pursued within the context of various faith traditions. Publications offered by the institute include *A Time to Speak: Faith Communities and Sexuality Education* and *A Time to Build: Creating Sexually Healthy Faith Communities*.

Soulforce
PO Box 3195, Lynchburg, VA   24503-0195
e-mail: info@soulforce.org
Web site: www.soulforce.org

The mandate of Soulforce is to help lesbian, gay, bisexual, and transgender people gain greater freedom from perceived persecution at the hands of conservative religious people who, according to the organization, misuse religion to oppress homosexuals. Publications offered by Soulforce include *Religion Gone Bad: The Hidden Dangers of the Christian Right, Christian Youth: An Important Voice in the Present Struggle for Gay Rights in America*, and *What the Bible Says—and Doesn't Say—About Homosexuality*.

U.S. Conference of Catholic Bishops
3211 Fourth St. NE, Washington, DC   20017

(202) 541-3000 • fax: (202) 541-3412
Web site: www.usccb.org

This is the official organization of the Catholic hierarchy in the United States. The purpose of the conference is to promote the programs and Biblical interpretations of the Church and carry out education and advocacy on various social issues based on Church doctrine and guidance. Publications produced by the Conference of Catholic Bishops include *Between Man and Woman, Human Sexuality*, and *Married Love and the Gift of Life.*

Bibliography

Books

Marilyn Bennett Alexander and James Preston	*We Were Baptized Too: Claiming God's Grace of Lesbians and Gays.* Louisville, KY: Westminster John Knox Press, 1996.
Erika Bachiochi, ed.	*The Cost of "Choice": Women Evaluate the Impact of Abortion.* New York: Encounter Books, 2004.
Donald Cozzens	*Freeing Celibacy.* Collegeville, MN: Liturgical Press, 2006.
William J. Doherty, et al.	*Why Marriage Matters: Twenty-One Conclusions from the Social Sciences.* New York: Institute for American Values, 2002.
J. Shoshannah Ehrlich	*Who Decides? The Abortion Rights of Teens.* Westport, CT: Praeger, 2006.
Fran Ferder and John Heagle	*Tender Fires: The Spiritual Promise of Sexuality.* New York: Crossroad, 2002.
Jeffrey Heskins	*Face to Face: Gay and Lesbian Clergy on Holiness and Life Together.* Grand Rapids, MI: William B. Eerdmans, 2006.
Patricia Beattie Jung, Mary E. Hunt, and Radhika Balakrishnan, eds.	*Good Sex: Feminist Perspectives from the World's Religions.* Piscataway, NJ: Rutgers University Press, 2000.

Erwin Lutzer	*The Truth About Same-Sex Marriage.* Chicago: Moody, 2004.
Daniel C. Maguire	*Sacred Choices: The Right to Contraception and Abortion in Ten World Religions.* Minneapolis, MN: Augsburg Fortress, 2001.
Kate Michelman	*With Liberty and Justice for All: A Life Spent Protecting the Right to Choose.* New York: Hudson Street Press, 2005.
Sydna Masse and Joan Phillips	*Her Choice to Heal: Finding Spiritual and Emotional Peace after Abortion.* Colorado Springs, CO: Chariot Victor, 1998.
Lisa Graham McMinn	*Sexuality and Holy Longing: Embracing Intimacy in a Broken World.* San Francisco: Jossey-Bass, 2004.
James Nelson and Sandra Longfellow, eds.	*Sexuality and the Sacred.* Louisville, KY: Westminster John Knox Press, 2006.
Mark D. Regnerus	*Forbidden Fruit: Sex and Religion in the Lives of American Teenagers.* New York: Oxford University Press, 2007.
C.K. Robertson, ed.	*Religion and Sexuality: Passionate Debates.* New York: Peter Lang, 2005.
Jack Rogers	*Jesus, the Bible, and Homosexuality: Explode the Myths, Heal the Church.* Louisville, KY: Westminster John Knox Press, 2005.

Katie Roiphe

Last Night in Paradise: Sex and Morals at the Century's End. Boston: Little, Brown, 1997.

Stephen J. Rossetti

The Joy of Priesthood. Notre Dame, IN: Ave Maria Press, 2005.

Kathleen M. Sands, ed.

God Forbid: Religion and Sex in American Public Life. New York: Oxford University Press, 2000.

Alexander Sanger

Beyond Choice: Reproductive Freedom in the 21st Century. New York: Public Affairs, 2004.

Wendy Shalit

A Return to Modesty: Discovering Lost Virtue. New York: Free Press, 1999.

David Shallenberger

Reclaiming the Spirit: Gay Men and Lesbians Come to Terms with Religion. Piscataway, NJ: Rutgers University Press, 1998.

Glenn T. Stanton

Marriage on Trial: The Case Against Same-Sex Marriage and Parenting. Downers Grove, IL: InterVarsity Press, 2004.

Leonore Tiefer

Sex Is Not a Natural Act and Other Essays. Colorado Springs, CO: Westview Press, 2004.

Mel White

Religion Gone Bad: The Hidden Dangers of the Christian Right. New York: Tarcher, 2006.

Lauren F. Winner   *Real Sex: The Naked Truth about Chastity*. Grand Rapids, MI: Brazos Press, 2006.

Naomi Wolf   *Promiscuities: The Secret Struggle for Womanhood*. New York: Random House, 1997.

Index